Music, Gender, and Sexuality Studies

Music, Gender, and Sexuality Studies: A Teacher's Guide serves as a guide to the professor tasked with teaching music to undergraduates, with a focus on gender. Although the notion of feminist approaches in musicology was once greeted with scorn, the last 40 years have seen a seismic shift across music studies, to the point that classes on women and music are now commonplace in most undergraduate music program. The goal of this book is to give the instructor some tools and strategies that will build confidence in approaching music as it relates to gender and sexuality, and to offer some advice on how to make the class rewarding for all.

The book is organized into four broad sections, plus an introduction outlining how to use the book and how the teaching of music, gender, and sexuality can be rewarding. Each section – Composition, Support, Performance, and Audience – includes possible themes for study and examples of music that can illuminate those themes, allowing the instructor to shape the course according to their own preference for classical, jazz, or popular styles. The author offers a practical guide to building syllabi that can fit the instructor's interests and the priorities of the institution, crafting assignments that will engage and inspire students, choosing repertoire from a range of styles and genres, and maintaining a focus on how music shapes gender, and how gender shapes music.

Jacqueline Warwick is a Professor of Musicology and Gender & Women's Studies at Dalhousie University in Canada.

Modern Musicology and the College Classroom
Series Editor: James A. Davis, SUNY Fredonia

Modern Musicology and the College Classroom is a series of professional titles for current and future college instructors of musicology in its broadest definition—encompassing music history, ethnomusicology, music theory, and music courses for all majors. Volumes feature a basic introduction to a significant field of current scholarship, a discussion of how the topic impacts pedagogical methodology and materials, and pragmatic suggestions for incorporating these ideas directly into the classroom.

Listening Across Borders
Musicology in the Global Classroom
Edited by James A. Davis and Christopher Lynch

Teaching Electronic Music
Cultural, Creative, and Analytical Perspectives
Edited by Blake Stevens

Race and Gender in the Western Music History Survey
A Teacher's Guide
Horace J. Maxile, Jr. and Kristen M. Turner

Music, Gender, and Sexuality Studies
A Teacher's Guide
Jacqueline Warwick

Music, Gender, and Sexuality Studies
A Teacher's Guide

Jacqueline Warwick

NEW YORK AND LONDON

First published 2023
by Routledge
605 Third Avenue, New York, NY 10158

and by Routledge
4 Park Square, Milton Park, Abingdon, Oxon, OX14 4RN

Routledge is an imprint of the Taylor & Francis Group, an informa business

© 2023 Taylor & Francis

The right of Jacqueline Warwick to be identified as author of this work has been asserted in accordance with sections 77 and 78 of the Copyright, Designs and Patents Act 1988.

All rights reserved. No part of this book may be reprinted or reproduced or utilized in any form or by any electronic, mechanical, or other means, now known or hereafter invented, including photocopying and recording, or in any information storage or retrieval system, without permission in writing from the publishers.

Trademark notice: Product or corporate names may be trademarks or registered trademarks, and are used only for identification and explanation without intent to infringe.

Library of Congress Cataloging-in-Publication Data
A catalog record for this title has been requested

ISBN: 978-0-367-48741-6 (hbk)
ISBN: 978-1-032-32844-7 (pbk)
ISBN: 978-1-003-04265-5 (ebk)

DOI: 10.4324/9781003042655

Typeset in Times New Roman
by KnowledgeWorks Global Ltd.

For Susan McClary, with love and thanks.

Contents

Acknowledgments   xi

Introduction   1
  Rationale 3
  Structure 4
  Sample Lesson One 6
    What Does Music Have to Do with Gender or Sexuality? 6
    Marked and Unmarked Identities 7
    Mainstream Musical Clichés of Gender 8
    Reflections and Connections: How Are Sounds Gendered? 11
  Notes 11
  Further Reading 12

1 Networks   13
  Suggested Topics 15
  Sample Lesson Two 16
    Salonnières 16
    Paris Salons and the Authority of the Amateur 16
    Pauline Viardot and French Romanticism 19
    The Musical Utopia of Nadezhda von Meck 20
    Reflections and Connections: Groupies and Rock Culture 21
  Sample Lesson Three 23
    African-American Women's Networks in the 1930s 23
    Florence Price, Estelle, and Margaret Bonds 24

    Marian Anderson and the Lincoln Memorial
       Concert 25
    Reflections and Connections: Women's Musical
       Networks in Other Regions 26
  Sample Lesson Four 27
    Womyn's Music Networks 27
    Maxine Feldman, Alix Dobkin, and the Birth of
       Women's Music 28
    Music and Lesbian Utopias 30
    The Michigan Women's Music Festival 31
    Reflections and Connections: The Emergence of
       TERF Rhetoric 33
  Discussion/Assignment Questions 34
  Notes 35
  Further Reading 37

2 Composition   38

  Suggested Topics 38
  Sample Lesson Five 39
    Symphonie Fantastique: Madness and
       Masculinity 39
    How Does Wordless Music Tell Stories? 40
    Hector Berlioz: Madness, Music, and Misogyny 41
    Harriet Smithson, Obsession, and the Idée Fixe 43
    Reflections and Connections: Echoes of Music and
       Madness 46
  Sample Lesson Six 46
    Blues Queens and Their Inheritors 46
    The Blues as Compositional Practice 47
    Bessie Smith, Empress of the Blues 49
    Ma Rainey and Outspoken Queerness 51
    Gladys Bentley, Harlem, and the Pansy Craze 52
    Reflections and Connections: Musical Heirs of the
       Blues Queens 53
  Sample Lesson Seven 54
    Motherhood 54
    Birth: A Universal Theme? 55
    Joni Mitchell, "Little Green" 56

Unwed Mothers and Magdalene Laundries 58
Sinéad O'Connor and Lost Pregnancy 60
Björk and the Corporeality of Mothering 61
Reflections and Connections: Shifting Attitudes
   Toward Motherhood 62
Discussion/Assignment Questions 63
Notes 64
Further Reading 66

3 Performance   68

Suggested Topics 69
Sample Lesson Eight 70
   Gender-bending Voices 70
   Castrati 70
   Travesti 73
   Pantomime Dames and Principal Boys 75
   Voices in Transition 76
   Reflections and Connections: Voicing Non-Binary
      Identities 77
Sample Lesson Nine 78
   Swan Lake 78
   Spectacle and Scopophilia 79
   Swan Lake: Story, Music, and Movement 80
   Swan Lake and Girl Culture 82
   Matthew Bourne's Swan Lake 83
   Connections and Reflections: Billy Elliot 84
Sample Lesson Ten 85
   Disney Musicals and Compulsory Heterosexuality 85
   Once Upon a Time: Snow White and the First Disney
      Princesses 87
   Cinderella and Sleeping Beauty 88
   Ariel and the Disney Renaissance 90
   Ideologies of Romance 91
   Disney Princesses Grappling with Diversity 92
   Reflections and Connections: Elsa and Anna 94
Discussion and Assignments Questions 95
Notes 95
Further Reading 98

4 Reception 99

    Suggested Topics 101
    Sample Lesson Eleven 101
        Lisztomania and Its Echoes 101
        Lisztomania 102
        Crooners 104
        Liberace, Manilow, and the Older Woman Fan 106
        Reflections and Connections: Kenny G and Smooth Jazz 107
    Sample Lesson Twelve 108
        Girlhood and Pop Music 108
        Girl Groups of the 1960s 109
        Girls in Rock Culture 112
        Reflections and Connections: Bedroom Pop and Girlhood 113
    Sample Lesson Thirteen 114
        Music and Sports 114
        Music, Sports, and Masculinity 114
        Boxing 116
        Improvisation and Individualism 117
        Collective Identity through Sports Fandom 118
        Reflections and Connections: Music in Other Communities 120
    Discussion/Assignment Questions 120
    Notes 121
    Further Reading 123

Index 124

Acknowledgments

This book grows out of my practice as a teacher in the university classroom. I was trained to do this work in a doctoral program that valued teaching as much as research, and I am grateful for the patient lessons and exemplary models of my mentors at UCLA. In serving as a Teaching Assistant to Robert Fink, Elisabeth LeGuin, Tamara Levitz, Susan McClary, Mitchell Morris, and Robert Walser, I had a front row seat to undergraduate teaching that ignited curiosity, made things make sense, and brought history alive.

May I also thank students at Dalhousie University who, over the years, have taught me to be a better teacher, particularly Jamie Blasina, Marc Blouin, Carolyn Brunelle, Gina Burgess, Lindsay Connolly, Jacob Danson-Faraday, Meredith Evans, Brittany Greening, Kavi Gunawardane, Emilie Hurst, Craig Jennex, Alexandra Killham, Artem Kolesov, Craig Lang, Mark MacAulay, Ryan McNutt, Maria Murphy, Clare Neil, Ntombi Nkiwane, Shannon Pringle, Isabelle Riche, Garrett Thorson, and Dilshan Weerasinghe. Their active minds, searching questions, and high standards challenged me to do my best in the classroom and outside it.

In preparing this manuscript, I have benefited from the guidance and encouragement of James Davis, and I thank him above all for convincing me to take this project on. Thanks also to Alexandra Carrico, Katie Grennell, Jared Miller, and Maria Murphy, who offered thoughtful feedback on drafts. I am grateful for the camaraderie of Horace Maxile, Angela Swift, and Kristen Turner, fellow-contributors to this series and to panel presentations about our work at the *Teaching Music History* conference and the annual meeting of the *American Musicological Society*, both in 2021.

My thinking about teaching, music, and writing is ever unfolding in dialogue with my partner, Steven Baur. Thank you for being my first, last, and best interlocutor.

Introduction

This book serves as a guide to the university instructor tasked with teaching an undergraduate class focused on music, gender, and sexualities. Although the notion of feminist approaches in musicology was greeted with scorn just a few decades ago ("Whatever next? Vegetarian musicology?"), classes on Women and Music are now commonplace in most university music programs. Indeed, the "women and music" model is by now out of touch with contemporary thinking about gender and sexuality, so the instructor assigned to the class may need careful guidance in order to teach in ways that serve their students' needs.

Let me be very clear, then, that this is *not* a guide to teaching a Women and Music class, and that in fact I advise against that approach. That model has become outdated, even damaging, now that we understand more about the great range of sexualities and gender identities that have always existed, and as we learn to challenge the gender binary. Our students' senses of gender and sexuality are as fluid and individual as their musical interests, and just as central to their understandings of themselves. Teaching music history with attention to gender and sexuality will enable your students to connect their musical lives with their gendered lives, leading to a greater understanding of music's tremendous cultural power and importance in human experience.

At many institutions, all music history classes are taught by a single music scholar, whose training and research interests may not involve gender-based approaches. In some places, a class like this may be offered as an alternative or update to a stale Music Appreciation course, in which case it may be assigned to an instructor whose expertise is in performance or music creation, not research. This person may strongly support gender equity, and be an expert in musical language, history, and repertoire, but these in themselves are not qualifications for teaching about how music reflects and directs gender conventions.

DOI: 10.4324/9781003042655-1

Is this you? You may well feel daunted, because the perils of getting it wrong in a class like this are more acute than those associated with teaching an incorrect conducting pattern or mislabeling a chord progression. Gender and sexuality are so central to a person's sense of self that a clumsy error can offend—and even harm—a student. Music can reinforce (or resist!) the hard lessons of patriarchy which injure us all. As bell hooks observes,

> The wounded child inside many males is a boy who, when he first spoke his truths, was silenced by paternal sadism, by a patriarchal world that did not want him to claim his true feelings. The wounded child inside many females is a girl who was taught from early childhood that she must become something other than herself, deny her true feelings, in order to attract and please others.[1]

Because of its unmatched ability to connect us to our emotions and our memories, music is a powerful force that can reopen these wounds. Teaching about music, gender, and sexuality requires courage and compassion, and a class like this presents an excellent opportunity to practice an ethics of care, as William Cheng urges us to do in all our work.[2]

Music plays a central role in constructing and negotiating our understandings of gender and sexuality as well as other aspects of identity. Just as we can all recognize—and respond to—musical representations of mood ranging from joy to rage, so we can also identify musical depictions of gender roles. Music is ephemeral and intangible, and we seem to experience it in our own bodies as it unfolds through time and space. Listeners may feel mystified by the specific techniques and strategies deployed in musical language, and efforts to understand why a particular song evokes such strong emotion can be frustrating; these barriers, in turn, serve to mystify music's power more. Musical instruments are themselves freighted with specific gender associations, so that it is commonplace to celebrate a guitar-playing woman as a rebel and to shame a flute-playing boy as a sissy. These reductive and harmful stereotypes function as well in the styles and strategies that musicians use; because music is an art form that represents people, it forges clichés of gender and race through sound.

In teaching about music, we often encounter the assumption that our goal is to make students love the repertoire and artists that we offer them, and that the music in our curriculum is there because we believe it is good. It is productive to teach problematic music and shift student mindsets away from believing that our job is to cultivate their listening tastes. We can show them that there is no "single scale of value" and that all music offers rewards and challenges shaped by its context. As Rob Walser advises, "instead of aestheticizing [particular] music, we should be historicizing all music and accounting in each case for the particular pleasures that are offered."[3]

I hope that my book will give you some tools and strategies to build your confidence in approaching music as it relates to gender and sexuality, making the class rewarding for everyone. Drawing on my years of experience teaching history surveys of classical and popular musics, gender studies classes that involve no music at all, and classes that bring music, gender, and sexuality together, for majors and non-majors alike, I offer you a guide to the term ahead. This book offers you methods for your teaching rather than content. My aim is to help you design a class that fits your interests and the priorities of your institution, while maintaining a focus on how music shapes gender, and how gender shapes music.

Rationale

These complexities and challenges mean that an adulatory history of women composers that runs parallel to—but rarely intersects with—the conventional lineage of "regular" composers, simply will not do. The goal should not be merely to recuperate women composers and add their names to the canon every student should know: rather, you have an opportunity to consider how gender conventions have governed access to musical training, opportunities to pursue careers in performance and composition, and other ways of participating in music activities. I encourage you to design your class not to stuff students full of repertoire, but to create time and space for them to contemplate and consider the shifting meanings of gender and sexuality as they are, and have been, represented in music. In committing to a sustained focus on gender, you can move away from a style of teaching that delivers lists, names, and facts at relentless speed.[4]

I believe that a maxim of "an inch wide and a mile deep" can be rewarding. I adhere to the philosophy of slow teaching, and to US historian Jane Simonsen's advice to "focus less on taking care of *what* students know and more on teaching students *how* to know, and 'what to do with the information [they] discover.'"[5] In this way I align, unsurprisingly, with the philosophy of my friend and mentor Susan McClary, who recommends that the music history teacher dispense with "fact-hoarding" of information for its own sake and organize teaching instead around a few key issues.[6]

Introduction

I also propose that composition not be the central lens through which to study music, gender, and sexuality. This is perhaps my most radical suggestion! The politics and ideologies of history have generally favored composers as the most (sometimes the only) important shapers of music; certainly, the music history I was taught was actually a history of composers, all presented as individual geniuses who worked in splendid isolation. This reductive cliché shapes many people's notions of what a composer is, and a narrative of composers begetting other composers (as it were) has always led to the overrepresentation of men in how we record music history.

In my own undergraduate education, I learned a very specific story about the history of music, which almost all occurred in Northern Europe. When I was a student, I genuinely believed that during the late 18th century, no one in the whole world was making music except for Haydn, Mozart, and Beethoven. I could not have named a single English composer of the period, much less talked about the rich and vibrant Indian music of the 18th century, and much, much less had any idea of what music was like during that time period in Toronto, where I was living. The history I was offered didn't acknowledge music from outside Europe until we came to the 20th century, as though the cultural traditions of all other countries in the world didn't begin until Europeans encountered them. The impact of this was to imply that only Europeans have history and complex development, an insidious, if unconscious, way of reinforcing the superiority of European culture and European people.

Finally, I am mindful of the fact that many students who are keenly interested in music are not literate in notation, and I hope to help you navigate this barrier. Those readers whose students can benefit from score study or transcription projects should, of course, include those tools in their teaching approaches. Because in-depth musical analysis involving score study is not appropriate in all classes, however, I will offer ways to talk about musical language and its effects that don't rely on notation.

Structure

The best course on gender and music will challenge notions of greatness by analyzing how gender has shaped musical canons in classical, popular, and vernacular styles. The "add women and stir" approach to music history suggests that women alone have gender, and that sexuality and race played no part in the careers of Bach, Beethoven, Brahms ... or the Beatles. But musicians do not exist in a vacuum, so

I advise you to explore the functions of gender and sexuality through four broad modules, in which composition does *not* come first.

This book is organized like the class on Music and Gender that I teach, with sections on Networks, Composition, Performance, and Reception. Of course, you may choose your own adventure in plotting your course, and you may prefer to explore all or only some of these themes, in whatever order makes sense to you. In each section, I theorize my approach to the concept at hand, I propose a few sample lecture topics, and I offer models for assignments, along with tips on adapting to suit students who are music majors or have no formal music training. Similarly, my examples are drawn from canonical to contemporary repertoires and figures, in classical, jazz, and popular music styles, so that you can shape your course according to your own priorities. Being the Toronto-raised, Los Angeles-educated daughter of British immigrants, I am most familiar with music cultures and gender conventions of the English-speaking world. I am addressing a reader also familiar with Euro-American canons, and I choose examples that will be accessible in that kind of sphere. I do not claim expertise in the diverse musics or complex gender issues of the entire world, so I will not presume to offer models drawn from beyond my familiarity. I hope, though, that parts of my theoretical framework can help instructors devise useful approaches to music cultures where they have expertise.

Treating the notion of networks first allows for a focus on musicians' relations, leading to a thorough understanding of the social realities of music making and the function of gender in constructing musical worlds, before proceeding to the study of individual musicians and their works. In this approach, I follow the model of Indigenous scholars and knowledge keepers, who warn against privileging individuals and losing sight of the social webs and networks that shape every person and their place in this world. This idea runs through a great deal of Indigenous scholarship; I encountered it first in TallBear's (2019) article "Caretaking Relations, Not American Dreaming," in which she offers an analytical framework of "being in good relation" that disrupts the grand narrative of exceptional individuals and their achievements. TallBear writes that "Thinking in terms of being in relation, I propose an explicitly spatial narrative of caretaking relations—both human and other-than-human—as an alternative to the temporally progressive settler-colonial American Dreaming that is every co-constituted with deadly hierarchies of life."[7] She states that asking "who are your relations?" is more important than asking "who are you?," and, along with scholars such as Dylan Robinson and Glen

Coulthard, TallBear asks us to recognize how community and geography shape cultures and people.

I hope it's easy to see how this insight can transform our approach to teaching music history, and why it may be particularly attractive to a teacher interested in equity. The instructor of a class on music, gender, and sexualities must be prepared to address students who listen to music from anywhere in the world anytime they want, and whose sense of gender and sexuality is as fluid and individual as their musical preferences. Students who ardently debate music and politics may sit beside students whose principal goal is to perform music, not contemplate its cultural value. Some will be activists well-versed in gender theory and cultural studies approaches; for others, even the notion that sex and gender are not the same thing may be a bewildering revelation.

In considering musical networks, you can help students to find the women and non-binary folks who have always been central to music-making, and to recognize the people and the work that are overlooked when we fixate myopically on genius and individual achievement. Our students' understanding of music as a social experience is deepened when we can help them to see the webs of relations and activities that support the existence of the music they love.

Sample Lesson One

What Does Music Have to Do with Gender or Sexuality?

However you choose to organize things, whichever module you being with, and whether you decide to focus only on canonical art music, contemporary popular music, or a diverse range of genres, your first lecture will be the most consequential in the course. In your first class meeting, you will set the tone for ensuing weeks; you will model the theoretical approaches to be used, and the kinds of questions to be asked. Consider also that this first meeting is the first time your students will meet one another, as well as meeting you. You can show them right from the start that they have things to learn from one another.

Some students in your group may be unsure that gender and sexuality have anything to do with musical sounds, much less that musical texts can be useful artifacts in teaching us about gender and sexuality. But whether or not your students recognize it, music is a force in all of their lives: it operates in our everyday experience to convey specific information about people. Even if your students are not trained musicians, they are highly sophisticated listeners. You can show them that they already know very well how to respond to musical cues, which are all the more powerful because we do not notice them at work.

For example, a film or television soundtrack tells us which characters are to be liked and hated, when to feel anxious, tender, triumphant, or angry, and whose happy ending to root for. You can easily illustrate this with reference to the theme music for a television sitcom that is well-known to your class, demonstrating how the familiar melody is altered in tempo and orchestration to suit plot developments ranging from somber to silly to sexy. The music does significant work in shaping understanding of the show's narrative; you can encourage them to test music's contributions by watching an episode with the sound turned off.

Music is also very effective in communicating information about tv characters in terms of their motives and their likability; more pertinently for our purposes, music helps us identify the gender of characters. In my own classes, I like to demonstrate this with an episode of the 1990s Swiss children's program *Pingu,* a clay animation series about an adorable penguin and his family; the series uses no identifiable language in its dialogue, so it relies on physical gesture and vocal intonation in its storytelling. In this unusual approach to communication, music is even more crucial than in texted stories.

The two-minute episode "Pingu the Superhero" (season 3, episode 17) contrasts the boisterous play of the boy penguin with the gentle play of his baby sister.[8] The musical score involves bombastic fanfares and crashing, syncopated rhythms for Pingu, and twinkling, music-box melodies for Pinga. These are well-worn tropes of male and female characters, instantly recognizable even on first viewing/hearing. Whether or not they remember *Pingu* from their own childhoods, students find the animation charming, and the ease with which they can identify gender stereotypes in the music bolsters confidence in their critical listening skills.

Marked and Unmarked Identities

The *Pingu* listening exercise can lead smoothly into a discussion of marked and unmarked identities, and the hegemonic assumptions that govern our shared notions of generic and particularized. The musical language of *Pingu* is only one strategy used to mark the characters on the basis of gender; the series creators also use visual markers, such as eyelashes, to distinguish the mother penguin from the father. This is a technique commonly used to mark feminine identities amongst animated characters (e.g., Minnie Mouse has eyelashes, Mickey does not) as well as stuffed animals and other toys. It is instructive to point out how these lessons about "proper" gender presentation begin to be imparted in childhood and to draw attention to the role that music

8   Introduction

plays in this teaching. It is also productive to help students recognize that unmarked identity is conventionally assumed to be male, white, cisgender, and heterosexual, while other identities must be marked and particularized.

Ask your class: what are the pitfalls inherent in this view? This exercise can prompt some discussion of what happens when we associate masculinity with normalcy, and the dangers of allowing unearned privileges to go unnoticed. To help them get comfortable contributing to class discussion, consider structuring time for small group conversations in response to the broad questions you throw out; each small group can elect a member who will report their ideas to the whole class.

When the conventionally masculine subject position is held to be synonymous with the default normal position, we find it more difficult to recognize the rights of other people to occupy that position, and we may even resist attempts at diversification (witness the discomfort with female, heroic protagonists in the action film genre, for example). Of course, many kinds of people are able to empathize with different kinds of protagonists, and can even see something of themselves reflected in a character who does not share their gender, sexuality, or race. However, straight, white men often struggle to do so, in part because they encounter so few opportunities to see themselves as anything but the central norm, anyone but the heroic protagonist. In discussion, ask students to consider the advantages and disadvantages of habitually expecting to identify with the norm.

In this first lecture, you should plan to advance some working definitions of terms such as sex, gender, sexuality, masculinity, and femininity. It may be exhilarating for your students to hear that these definitions will be subject to change through the semester! You may feel most comfortable defining "sex" in terms of the biological, anatomical apparatuses that mark bodies as male or female, while "gender" refers to the cultural meanings of maleness and femaleness. Be sure to remind your students that human bodies of all genders are more alike than they are different, and that they do not all fit into the male/female binary which has been used to categorize people into hegemonic roles and to develop unequal power relations.

Mainstream Musical Clichés of Gender

While I'm aware of the dangers of seeming reductive, I do find it useful to begin with identifying the most dominant, mainstream concepts, prompting students to understand these definitions are no more natural or immutable than others. Thus, I offer them sociologist Goffman's (1963) take on hegemonic masculinity:

> In an important sense there is only one complete unblushing male in America: a young, married, white, urban, northern, heterosexual, Protestant, father, of college education, fully employed, of good complexion, weight, and height, and a recent record in sports [...] Any male who fails to qualify in any of these ways is likely to view himself—during moments at least—as unworthy, incomplete, and inferior ...[9]

Ask your students to discuss which parts of this definition continue to hold sway; is it a yardstick of masculinity that they recognize? This can lead to reflection about how this vision of masculinity lines up with clichés outside the USA, and whether all aspects identified by Goffman retain their power in your current historical moment.

This most conventional notion of white, male, straight, and cisgender identity is a good place to begin teaching this kind of critical thinking, precisely because students will recognize its cultural clout but will also have had few opportunities to unpack its meanings through a teacher-led dialogue. This discussion will inevitably lead to the realization that definitions of masculinity are not fixed, but rather are historically and geographically situated. This realization, in turn, makes it easier for students to understand how all gender identities are—and always have been—constructed to fit the exigencies of their social contexts. Furthermore, social rules about gender have always governed the ways that gender is presented in music, so that music creation and performance must always be in relation to hegemonic norms and distributions of power.

And how do musical sounds depict dominant masculinity? When we consider the hero protagonist, what kinds of music do we imagine accompanying him? It's easy to explore this idea with reference to major action film soundtracks that are familiar to your students. Whether you choose to play Elfman's *Batman* score, Fiedel's *Terminator* theme, Marvel's *Avengers* themes (Silvestri), or John Williams's work for films such as *Superman, Star Wars, Raiders of the Lost Ark* (among others), you will be dealing with music that deploys horn fanfares, syncopated rhythms, strings used percussively, and spacious textures. Encourage your students to identify why these sounds are recognized as heroic and manly, and to consider how they reinscribe the idea that personality traits of courage, conviction, and authority are straight-, white-, and male-coded. What kinds of alterations tend to be made to create an orchestral score ascribing valor and confidence to a white female hero, such as Marvel's Captain Marvel, or a Black male hero, such as Marvel's Black Panther?

A focus on orchestral soundtracks to major blockbuster films is a good way to find common ground amongst your students, and this is especially valuable if the class comprises music majors and nonmajors. You can choose specific movie themes that will be familiar, and the recognition will be reassuring to students who may feel insecure about a lack of formal music background. This topic will also be heartening to those students majoring in performance in classical music repertoires, who may feel anxious about a class that stretches their critical listening and interpretive skills rather than their playing technique. If your class is going to cover repertoire from multiple genres of classical and popular music (which I recommend), a lesson on orchestral film scores will also gently make it clear that some popular music draws very faithfully on the language of canonical European composers such as Strauss, Mahler, Holst, and Prokofiev.

Not by coincidence, this musical representation of (white male) heroism is also common in the themes for television news broadcasts. Indeed, in 1985, John Williams himself wrote the themes for NBC News in the United States, creating a package of cues and themes which provided musical coherence among the network's news programs for several decades. Canadian musicologist James Deaville observes that "Williams's traditional, stately theme, replete with the requisite brass fanfares to establish authority and scurrying strings to emulate the teletype and the busy news office, set a standard for ABC, CBS, and—above all—CNN."[10] A brief tour of examples from CNN to BBC to Fox News to Al Jazeera may prompt discussion about the musical language of manly confidence, and the appeal of this sonic representation of authority across various communities.

Some of your students will be more familiar with musical depictions of heroism in rock culture, where horn fanfares are replaced by guitar solos, and where heroes are more likely to be cast as outlaw rebels than as saviors. If there are innumerable film scores and orchestral works about heroes kicking against rigid social expectations, such as Beethoven's 3rd Symphony or Richard Strauss's *Ein Heldenleben,* then rock'n'roll and rock genres are positively teeming with works in the same vein, from Dion's "The Wanderer" to the Allman Brothers' "Ramblin' Man," Pink Floyd's "The Wall," Bruce Springsteen's "Born to Run" to Green Day's "Boulevard of Broken Dreams." Songs like these draw on the notion of the artist as a rebellious figure who resists the smothering confines of domesticity, and it should be possible to help your students see how this cliché tends to conflate women with dreary obligations and ennui, while rock'n'roll freedom is depicted as the domain of men.

Reflections and Connections: How Are Sounds Gendered?

Finally, ask your students to think about whether musical sounds and instruments are themselves gendered. If you have implemented small group discussions throughout this first class, they may by now be comfortable enough to consider this question *en masse*. With prepared images and/or short sound clips of common instruments such as trumpet, flute, electric guitar, drum kit, and harp, you can end the class with a lively conversation that elicits some personal anecdotes. I am sorry to report that I have never run this discussion without hearing a story along the lines of a girl whose band teacher directed her to clarinet instead of trombone, or a boy dissuaded from picking up the flute. Although it's disappointing to acknowledge that these sexist ideologies continue to determine choices in young people's lives, these anecdotes do demonstrate vividly the part that music plays in policing gender roles. Confronting them underscores the value of a class on music, gender, and sexualities, and can create a climate in which students are able to connect their own experiences to hegemonic norms.

Notes

1. bell hooks, *All About Love: New Visions* (New York: HarperCollins, 2000), 49.
2. William Cheng, *Just Vibrations: The Purpose of Sounding Good* (Ann Arbor: University of Michigan Press, 2016).
3. Robert Walser, "Popular Music Analysis: Ten Apothegms and Four Instances," in Allan Moore, ed., *Analyzing Popular Music* (Cambridge: Cambridge University Press, 2009), 16–38: 19–20.
4. For inspiring advice on slow teaching, see Fred Everett Maus, "Teaching Music Slowly," in Stephannie Gearhart and Jonathan Chambers, *Reversing the Cult of Speed in Higher Education: The Slow Movement in the Arts and Humanities* (New York: Routledge, 2019): 209–24.
5. Jane Simonsen, "Consuming Time or Making Time?" in Stephanie S. Gearhart and Jonathan Chambers, eds., *Reversing the Cult of Speed in Higher Education: The Slow Movement in the Arts and Humanities* (New York: Routledge, 2019), 196–208: 193.
6. Susan McClary, "Foreword," in James A. Davis, *The Music History Classroom* (Aldershot, UK: Ashgate, 2016): xii.
7. Kim TallBear, "Caretaking Relations, Not American Dreaming," *Kalfou* Vol. 6/1, Spring 2019, 24–41: 25.

8. "Pingu Plays Superhero," *Pingu* season 3, episode 17 (1996), seen at *Pingu Official Channel* https://www.youtube.com/watch?v=ys8ksItl2vU, accessed October 13, 2021.
9. Erving Goffman, *Stigma: Notes on the Management of Spoiled Identity* (New York: Simon and Schuster, 1963), 128.
10. James Deaville, "The Changing Sounds of War: Television News Music and Armed Conflicts from Vietnam to Iraq," in Susan Fast and Kip Pegley, eds., *Music, Politics, and Violence* (Middletown, CT: Wesleyan University Press, 2012), 104–26: 114.

Further Reading

Maggie, Berg and Barbara K. Seeber. *The Slow Professor: Challenging the Culture of Speed in the Academy*. Toronto: University of Toronto Press, 2016.

Cheng, William. *Just Vibrations: The Purpose of Sounding Good*. Ann Arbor: University of Michigan Press, 2016.

Citron, Marcia. "Gender, Professionalism, and the Musical Canon," *Journal of Musicology* 8/1 (Winter, 1990): 102–17.

Goffman, Erving. *Stigma: Notes on the Management of Spoiled Identity*. New York: Simon and Schuster, 1963.

Gearhart, Stephanie and Jonathan Chambers. *Reversing the Cult of Speed in Higher Education: The Slow Movement in the Arts and Humanities*. New York: Routledge, 2021.

Penny, Laurie. "What to Do When You're Not the Hero Anymore," *The New Statesman (UK Edition)*, December 28, 2015. https://www.newstatesman.com/culture/2015/12/what-do-when-youre-not-hero-any-more

Press, Joy and Simon Reynolds. *The Sex Revolts: Gender, Rebellion, and Rock'n'Roll*. Cambridge, MA: Harvard University Press, 1995.

Robinson, Dylan. *Hungry Listening: Resonant Theory for Indigenous Sound Studies*. Minneapolis: University of Minnesota Press, 2020.

TallBear, Kim. "Caretaking Relations, Not American Dreaming," *Kalfou* 6/1 (Winter, 2019): 24–41.

Waugh, Linda. "Marked and Unmarked: A Choice Between Unequals in Semiotic Structure," *Semiotica* 38/3-4 (Winter, 1982): 299–318.

1 Networks

In 2017, the US scholar and novelist Bruce Holsinger created a Twitter hashtag, #thanksfortyping, which documented instances of male authors using their books' acknowledgements sections to thank their (invariably unnamed) wives for typing, editing, transcribing, and other work essential to the production of their scholarship. Holsinger's examples shed light on the invisible labor of women, and they simultaneously illuminated the toil necessary to gather ideas into coherence. This unglamorous work is not consistent with the image of a brilliant thinker whose insights fall perfectly formed onto the page, so acknowledging its existence—and its value—complicates our preferred notions of both genius and gender.

When we consider the full array of chores involved in creating the conditions required to produce art, from editing to network-building to childcare, we can more easily see the team of workers who enable the artist. Famously, Sophia Tolstoy copied out *War and Peace* eight times—by hand!—while also bearing 13 children and overseeing the operations of the Tolstoy household and staff. Jenny Marx, who had relinquished her status as a baroness in order to dedicate her life to social revolution, helped her husband Karl to develop his ideas, rewrote his barely decipherable notes, and used her personal contacts to raise funds to support his work while also struggling to keep their children alive in often-desperate poverty. How might Tolstoy's and Marx's thought process and literary output have been different if not for their wives' support and management of stressful demands on their time?

In the sphere of music history, our blinkered focus on composers often distorts understanding how artistic reputations were and are constructed. If we fail to acknowledge Clara Schumann's tireless efforts to promote her husband's compositions through her prodigious concert

DOI: 10.4324/9781003042655-2

career, we have misunderstood him and his place in history. When we give serious attention to Alma Mahler's role as an artistic interlocutor and muse to her husband Gustav (and subsequent husbands Walter Gropius and Franz Werfel, as well as other artists including Oskar Kokoshka), instead of trivializing her as a man-hungry socialite and *femme fatale*, we gain a better grasp on the vibrant, interdisciplinary arts scene of *fin-de-siècle* Vienna. When we consider that Cosima Wagner—who died in 1930, having outlived her husband by nearly 40 years—made it her life's work to preserve and promote his music, we understand better how Wagner's vision of German cultural heritage was accessible to the creators of Nazi ideology in the 1920s. And if we examine the dynamics of Louis Armstrong's artistic collaborations with his second wife, pianist Lil Hardin, we see more clearly how jazz became the height of sophistication and glamour in US cities during that same decade.

This chapter aims to help you illuminate the muses, patrons, spouses, and others whose labor makes it possible for artists to create. Examining musical networks, whether in the 18th-century salon culture or in rock groupiedom of the 1960s and 1970s, places musicians among their relations, and thus affords a truer portrayal of their work. In teaching your students to deploy what US philosopher Nancy Hartsock has called a feminist standpoint, you can help them develop a deeper understanding of the social realities of music making, and the functions of sex and gender in constructing musical worlds.

Consider how servants in a stately home (or in a soap opera about a stately home!) know both their own cultural sphere and the sphere of the aristocrats they attend "upstairs," while the aristocrats are wholly ignorant of the downstairs world. In this analogy, the servant's standpoint reveals the most complete truth. Hartsock's 1983 essay "The Feminist Standpoint: Developing the Ground for a Specifically Feminist Historical Materialism," develops the philosophical concept of standpoint epistemology, which builds on Hegel's analysis of the master–slave relationship and recognizes that knowledge and other forms of power are socially positioned. This means that people positioned at the margins often know more than those at the center.

In seeking to understand power, Hartsock asserts that questions should start from the standpoint of women, because they know the world of men, and their view of social structures also reveals truths imperceptible to men. She writes that "women's experience not only inverts that of men but forms a basis on which to expose abstract masculinity as both partial and fundamentally perverse, as not only occupying only one side of the dualities it has constructed but reversing the proper valuation of human activity."[1] Hartsock, a white American scholar, was writing in the midst of significant critiques of power, including the landmark Combahee River Collective Statement of 1977: this work was created by a Boston-based group of Black feminist lesbian writers who drew attention to the interlocking, intersecting systems of oppression that could not be fully addressed by either white feminism or Black civil rights activism.[2] Just so, following Hartsock and the Combahee River Collective, we may conclude that the worldview of straight, cisgender, white men is partial and distorted.

When we apply this model to the world of music and recognize that only limited realities are visible from the standpoints of composers or performers, we can begin to see and hear differently. If nothing else, the lesson of the feminist standpoint teaches students the necessity of considering more than one perspective. Not incidentally, this lens on musical creation will make it easier for us to find women and non-binary people whose contributions to art have been minimized. However, teaching a module on musical networks can do more than recuperate the erased labor of those women adjacent to Great Men; through consideration of musical networks, we can illuminate the processes and communities that support all musicians, and we can begin to correct the distortions of reductive histories of music.

Suggested Topics

This module of a course provides you with the opportunity to teach about people habitually overlooked or erased in conventional histories of music and to re-evaluate the importance of muses, sound engineers, concert promoters, and hostesses. In the following pages, I'll share guidelines for possible lessons on figures and networks who have contributed to music across a few genres, beginning with the European salon culture of the 19th century, touching on the networks of Black women in early 20th-century United States, and also visiting the music of the 1970s womyn's movement. Through these topics, you can help your students to recognize the important webs of support that all musicians rely on in order to create. You can also help them to understand the additional barriers that have faced women seeking to participate in music cultures, and to see how specific women were resourceful enough to carve out places for themselves. Although the case studies I have chosen focus principally on women, I hope that the models can inspire consideration of other possible networks in music.

Sample Lesson Two

Salonnières

In her 2007 study of the English composer Edward Elgar's relationship to salon culture, British musicologist Sophie Fuller documents the under-examined, vibrant musical sphere of private English homes that was led largely by upper-class and upper-middle-class women at the end of the 19th century. In a footnote, Fuller notes that music historians have tended to overlook the activities and inner workings of this world, and she observes tartly that "In the world view of these scholars, it was only the public, masculine musical spaces that were worth investigating. Feminized spaces were simply assumed to be trivial, frivolous, and insignificant."[3] Fuller's careful attention to privileged, amateur music making recovers the important roles of women like Mary Gladstone (daughter of prime minister William Gladstone) as well as of queer men like Frank Schuster. These were highly skilled musicians, patrons, and critics who used their wealth and standing to contribute significantly to England's musical life, but their activities have been minimized in most histories.

Fuller's study demonstrates how disregard for feminized spaces actually leads to a distorted understanding of artistic process, aesthetics, and social structures. Furthermore, in a study of two 19th-century hostesses (Mary Gladstone and Annie Fields) and their roles in cultivating literary tastes in England and New England, respectively, Susan Harris neatly summarizes the complexities of the hostess role, observing that hostesses were recognized as important shapers of culture even though their official status was subordinate to their husbands or fathers. Harris considers the elite group of Anglo-American women "who first learned how to create and manage a domestic environment in which the business of influencing others was the major occupation, and who subsequently took their skills into the realms of public philanthropy and the building of cultural institutions."[4] Officially and legally, these salon hostesses were second-class citizens, yet they supported artists, trained audiences, and laid the foundations of modern public cultural life. Their activities could not be recognized as work in their day, yet by today's standards, they achieved successful and impressive careers.

Paris Salons and the Authority of the Amateur

Although the term "salonnière" is most commonly associated with the circle of aristocratic hostesses who supported the development of Enlightenment thinking and founding of institutions such as the

Academie française in the 17th and 18th centuries, the idea of the salon was of vital importance to musicians and other artists long afterwards. Indeed, with the deterioration of the patronage system that had ensured steady employment for composers such as Haydn, musicians from the 19th century onward have had to seek out commissions, teaching jobs, paying performance opportunities, and other forms of support from members of the public.

Often, this has meant forming relationships with wealthy women. For their part, these women seek out promising musical talent in order to accrue social capital through their philanthropy and discerning tastes. Hostesses have done valuable work in cultivating vibrant, knowledgeable arts communities as well as in providing guidance and support for those artists who interested them. Fuller and Harris show that salon hostesses at the end of the 19th century were typically highly educated, sophisticated thinkers, and skilled musicians, whose upbringing had involved the cultivation of ladylike accomplishments such as European languages, painting, and music performance and creation. In terms of musicianship specifically, it is clear that an extremely high level of proficiency was expected.

This will be a startling idea for many students, accustomed as they are to assuming that amateurs are, by definition, less skilled than professionals. Many will assume also that a person who practices diligently to maintain technique must aspire to a professional career in music. Within the highest social circles, however, the value of excellent musicianship has been seen as entirely separate from the drudgery of life as a working musician. The women—and many of the men—studied by Fuller would have recoiled from the prospect of performing for a paying public. The life of a working musician, after all, offered fewer comforts and less autonomy than that of a wealthy music connoisseur. For musicians of bourgeois and upper-class backgrounds, musical was an important accomplishment, but private, amateur performance was the most attractive option. So, a serious, nuanced consideration of salon music culture and the women who curated it will require students to let go of a seldom-examined prejudice about amateur musicians. This in itself will lead to new ways of thinking about music and about gender.

Similarly, although the term "salon music" is often used in a disparaging way, implying repertoire that is light, trite, and sentimental, the opposite may be true: salons provided forums in which professional composers could experiment with daring material. Here, they could take risks and receive thoughtful feedback while making tamer repertoire choices for the less sophisticated audiences of the public concert hall. As British conductor James Ross notes in an article about

French salons of the 19th century: "salons offered an alternative and non-commercial setting for serious performance. They were a haven for the new and the controversial, and were central to French understanding and eventual acceptance of Wagner in the 1880s and 1890s."[5] Ross provides several examples of figures such as Debussy sharing work in progress at Paris salon evenings, and he notes that these private concerts served both to help a composer refine their work before public performance, and also to "prepare influential theatre-goers and win support before a première."[6]

Music salons were training grounds for audiences as well as composers and performers, providing arenas for serious music lovers to share their passions and air their ideas in safe, respectable environments. Some salons were highly prestigious, and invitations were sought after by aspiring musicians for the entrées they would provide into high society. Ross writes that the salon of the legendary Princess Mathilde Bonaparte (1820–1904) was "a court in itself" and "the home and centre of Parisian intellect," through which she influenced artistic developments through her own and her friends' patronage.[7] Within a sphere designed and controlled by its hostess, bright, ambitious women could perform music and discuss musical ideas alongside the leading composers, critics, and performers of their community. The élite women who exerted influence in this realm were powerful; they could even require their guests to uphold strict etiquette, such as imposing silence during musical performance when this was not yet standard at public concerts.[8]

Because being a good hostess was (and is!) a crucial skill for upper and upper-middle-class women, salons offered an attractive way for a creative and ambitious woman to participate in the Romantic art movement. A good hostess could create an environment in which artists would feel at ease, and her introductions could facilitate connections between artists. Without compromising her reputation or disrupting hegemonic ideals of women's place in the home, she could direct conversation and contribute to the exchange of ideas, foster collaborative relationships, and observe the creative process from a front-row seat. To be sure, the 19th-century society hostess is easy to caricature as frivolous and of feeble artistic talent. Emma Thompson's performance in the 1991 film *Impromptu* serves as an example: as the fictitious Duchess d'Antan, whose country estate party brings together real luminaries of the French arts scene Frédéric Chopin, Franz Liszt, Eugène Delacroix, Alfred de Musset, and Georges Sand (Aurore Dudevant), she fawns over her artist guests, and the audience is encouraged to despise her breathless attempts at conversation. This type of characterization appeals because it reinforces the Romantic notion of Artists-with-a-capital-A, beings whose profundity and brilliance could never be contained by dreary social mores, and whose ideas and ideals are far beyond the comprehension of a mere housewife, no matter how wealthy. In reality, a woman operating in the role of salon hostess would have to be well-read and intelligent, and her ideas and opinions would be treated with respect and serious attention (by those who hoped for further invitations, at least). Many salonnières attained a level of agency and authority that was far beyond what a working artist could hope for, and a skilled hostess would take satisfaction in seeing the traces of her influence in the careers of her protegés.

Pauline Viardot and French Romanticism

One of the most successful Parisian hostesses of the late 19th century was Pauline Garcìa Viardot (1821–1910), whose fame has endured largely because of her own achievements as a professional singer and respected amateur composer. Born into a family of distinguished singers originally from Spain, Viardot took piano lessons from Franz Liszt, played duets with Chopin, and became a protégée of Georges Sand, the infamous baroness who published novels under a man's name and enjoyed tempestuous love affairs with Chopin and other artists. The particularities of Viardot's singing career are themselves of interest in the terms of gender expectations, as many contemporary accounts indicate her success was hampered by her looks. Unlike her more famous sister, Maria Garcìa Malibran (1808–1836), Pauline did not conform to contemporary standards of beauty, then (as now) important aspects of a singer's appeal. Had she been prettier, she might have been too busy with a stage career to achieve the kind of influence that allowed her to shape a generation of French composers.

At the age of 18, upon Sand's advice, she married the journalist, translator, and theatre producer Louis Viardot, dull and some 21 years her senior, but able to offer her financial stability. The couple became known for their twice-weekly salons, in their Paris home as well as their country estate, over which Pauline presided and offered artistic stimulation and guidance to figures such as Hector Berlioz, Richard Wagner, Johannes Brahms (who wrote his "Alto Rhapsody" for her toward the end of her singing career), Jules Massenet, Giacomo Meyerbeer, and Gabriel Fauré. The fabled Thursday soirées were forums for composers to try out new musical ideas (Sunday afternoons were more relaxed occasions, only for the Viardots' most intimate circle), and Pauline

Viardot became a crucial mentor and advocate for many. In the case of Charles Gounod, who referred to her as "the godmother of my career," she made her own contract renewal at the Paris Opera conditional on Gounod's opera *Sapho* being commissioned.[9] Furthermore, when the young composer suffered a family tragedy, she offered her summer home as a retreat where he could regain his focus.[10] Gabriel Fauré paid tribute to her in numerous song dedications, and she was also the dedicatee of large-scale works such as Camille Saint-Saëns's 1877 opera *Samson et Dalila*.

In middle and late years, after retiring from the stage, Viardot took greater interest in music from beyond Paris. Drawing on her own expertise as a singer and speaker of Russian, she was enthusiastic about Russian music, and she presented many songs by Pyotr Ilyich Tchaikovsky (1840–1893) at her salon; her endorsement helped to generate interest in his music in Parisian circles.

The Musical Utopia of Nadezhda von Meck

The great benefactor of Tchaikovsky's career, of course, was Nadezhda von Meck (1831–1894), a Russian woman who eschewed Viardot's style of salon but nevertheless was a dedicated supporter of the arts. Von Meck grew up in a privileged, music-loving household and married respectably in her teens, thereafter taking an active interest in her husband's career and encouraging him to invest in the railway system being built in Russia. This venture led to great wealth, money that von Meck managed herself when she became a widow in her mid-40s.[11]

In widowhood, she became reclusive and saw few people apart from her 11 (surviving) children and their families, so salon gatherings with acquaintances and strangers would have been anathema to her. At the same time, she took a keen interest in music and supported a small group of musicians who stayed at her estate and offered regular performances for her and her family's enjoyment. Through engaging young, up-and-coming musicians, von Meck was able to keep pace with artistic currents in major cities, and her patronage offered these players retreat-like experiences, either at her comfortable home near Smolensk or in vacation homes elsewhere in Europe. The ensemble included the 18-year-old Claude Debussy, whom she hired as a piano teacher for her children and a duet partner for herself over three summers, in France and Italy as well as at the family home in Russia.[12] Debussy was so enthralled by the von Meck family and their lifestyle that he sought marriage with the 16-year-old daughter, Sophie (who declined), and he wept when he had to return to his studies in Paris.[13]

This kind of arrangement is scarcely comprehensible by today's standards, but it was a reasonably common way for wealthy Russian families of the time to have music on demand in their homes. Von Meck's ensemble was unusual only in that she had excellent taste, discerning enough to hire talents such as Nikolai Rubinstein, and the ability to create an atmosphere in which these musicians flourished and developed. Her withdrawal from public life, then, was perhaps more like living in a bespoke artist's colony than a retreat into isolation and gloom.

Tchaikovsky came to von Meck's attention when "her" violinist, his former student Iosif Kotek, hired the composer to write arrangements for chamber concerts at her home. Although the two never met in person (by her strict wish), von Meck and Tchaikovsky wrote to one another for 14 years, and she provided him with a salary that allowed him to give up his teaching position at the Moscow Conservatory. The letters between them represent a lively exchange of ideas between well-matched minds, and a relationship that was emotionally important and artistically stimulating to both. Recognizing the value of this correspondence to both participants helps us to see the web of activity that surrounds and supports the creation of musical work.

The copious correspondence between Tchaikovsky and von Meck reveals the fervid, sometimes erotically charged connection between them, underscoring the passionate nature of music and its function in our inner lives. For Tchaikovsky, an introvert whose direct personal relationships were famously disastrous, writing to von Meck offered a way to explore his most intimate feelings and to rehearse expressing them through the language of music. Readers may laugh or cringe at the intensity of emotion in the letters, and it has been tempting to deride Nadezhda von Meck as sentimental and fannish, sighing over the letters of a pop idol to whom she meant little more than a pay cheque.[14] But serious and respectful consideration, that acknowledges the immense value of a high-level interlocutor to an artist in developing ideas, can reveal von Meck to be an intelligent, thoughtful music lover who lived life on her own terms. When we can recognize her as such, we see more easily her immeasurable importance to Tchaikovsky and to the very development of Russian music.

Reflections and Connections: Groupies and Rock Culture

The theme of passionate attachment via music is also central to the discourse around "groupies," the young female fans who were central to rock music culture in the late 20th century. As with Romanticism, the music in question involved themes of intense emotion, rebellion against stuffy social rules, and the notion of the misunderstood, tormented artist yearning for connection. After the development of reliable, accessible birth control and before the onset of the AIDS epidemic, the 1970s were a brief window of time during which sex was virtually risk-free. In this period, rock songs could be much more direct about sex and desire than artists could have been in the 19th century. Also, the possibility of listening to the same recordings in homes around the world meant that rock music played a crucial role in sexual awakening for an entire generation of youth. This included girls and young women who found themselves in the songs and then sought out the singers.

Groupies were viewed with horrified fascination because of their unbridled sexuality and aggressive pursuit of connection with the artists who spoke to them through their music. Groupiedom was a way for girls and women to connect with the music that mattered so much to them, and they organized networks to provide practical, emotional, and sexual hospitality to traveling musicians. US music critic Ann Powers notes:

> This is what the groupie system provided. A hardworking band could pull into a new town and expect to be greeted by young women, who, like wartime nurses, would offer them succor. In return, those women would gain status in a world where few other roles were available—there were barely any females onstage, on the road crew, in management, or working in positions of power at the venues. Becoming a groupie placed women in rock on a kind of solid ground, however imaginary it ultimately proved.[15]

White feminist scholars such as Lisa Rhodes and Norma Coates have shown that much of the hostility directed at groupies was an attempt to stifle their power in a scene which relied on them even as it reviled them. The presence of attractive and adoring girls and women was an essential aspect of life in rock music (and, of course, other musics), and many of these attained renown for their roles as confidantes, muses, and mentors. In the rock music press, groupiedom was simultaneously decried as pathetic flunkeydom and promoted as a glamorous sort of career, with magazines offering advice to teens on how to meet rock stars but also reveling in the humiliations of famous groupies such as Pamela des Barres. Also, Coates observes that "the presence of groupies on the rock scene also helps to expunge the specter of homosexuality that haunts the homosociality of rock music performance and male fandom."[16] With a steady stream of girls being taken conspicuously to bed and then left cheerfully behind when the musicians moved on, rock culture found an easy way to dispel anxieties about the machismo of men who would willingly prance and preen on stage, making spectacles of themselves.

Clearly, the role of the groupie was complex and delicate. Above all, the groupie of rock culture and the hostess of Romantic music salons were rare examples of women with any agency and authority in music's inner circles. Although neither path was without its risks and disappointments, salonnières and groupies were able to immerse themselves into music, interacting intimately with musicians and observing creative processes from an insider's standpoint. The musicians who encountered their generosity of spirit benefitted in direct ways, and their role in forging music cultures should not be underestimated.

Sample Lesson Three

African-American Women's Networks in the 1930s

Consideration of African-American composer Florence Price (1887–1953) and the networks of Black women who enabled her artistic life can provide a celebratory example of a musical community that navigated the double burdens of racism and sexism. The best way into this kind of lesson is to begin with the network of performers who interpreted Price's work. For music students accustomed to thinking of performers as servants to the composer's intentions, it may be novel and refreshing to think about how an established performer can actually elevate a composer's profile. For students not indoctrinated in the hierarchies of Western Art Music history, however, it will be easier to understand that a music star has the power to make or break a songwriter. Some of them may be familiar with the example of African-American songwriter Vincent Berry, who was living in his car when Beyoncé recorded his ballad "Sandcastles" on her 2016 album *Lemonade*.[17]

Pianist Margaret Bonds and singer Marian Anderson were both instrumental in supporting the career of Florence Price. Each of these women had considerable social and artistic capital which they were able to deploy to lift up Price's talent and ambition, without her having herself to disrupt middle-class notions of ladylike demureness, modesty, and reticence about accomplishments. The roles of these performers can lead to consideration of musicians' collectives, both formal and informal, and to a recognition of the ways that Black women form networks to navigate institutional racism and sexism.

Florence Price, Estelle, and Margaret Bonds

It makes sense to begin the lesson with a biographical sketch of Price from a feminist standpoint, drawing on the work of US musicologists Rae Linda Brown, Douglas Shadle, and Alisha Lola Jones. Price was born into relative privilege in Little Rock, the daughter of a middle-class family who supported her musical interests, including formal studies at the New England Conservatory. Her father died when she was in her early 20s, at which point her mother took advantage of her light skin and vanished into a life as a white woman, severing all contact with her daughter—at this relatively young age, Florence was alone in the world. She married Little Rock solicitor Thomas Price, had three children, and was able to hire a live-in nanny who freed up time for Florence to teach, compose, and participate in the city's musical life. When the family moved to Chicago, however, her husband's career faltered while Florence's star rose. The marriage deteriorated into abuse and eventual divorce, leaving her with custody of the two children still living at home. A feminist lens can help students to see how patriarchal family hierarchy might be destabilized by a wife's ambition and talent, and the threat this would pose to her husband as head of the household.

Though her career went from success to success in the 1930s, a second marriage also broke down, causing Price and her teenage daughters to move in with Margaret Bonds and her mother Estelle. This woman-led family residence was an important hub for Black artists in Chicago, as divorcée Estelle Bonds was the hostess of a legendary artist salon. Margaret Bonds claimed that "From my mother, I had actual physical contact with all living composers of African descent ... my mother had a collector's nose for anything that was artistic."[18] At this house and under the watchful eye of this hostess, Price met distinguished figures such as Langston Hughes, and she was able to nurture artistically collaborative relationships without compromising her respectability.

It is worthwhile to consider the roles of women like Estelle Bonds in constructing the social milieux that allowed artists to meet, draw inspiration from one another, and nurture creativity, much like the salonnières discussed above. This can lead to some fruitful discussion about the ways that women's participation in music continues to be circumscribed; there were and are genuine and significant dangers of assault in nightclubs, dressing rooms, tour busses, and other music workspaces. A salon like Estelle Bonds's offered a safe, respectable space where Price could let her guard down and focus on the exchange of ideas.

Price took a keen interest in nurturing the musical talent of young Margaret Bonds, who reciprocated by performing as soloist in her piano concerto. The creation history of this work itself owes a great deal to networks of women, as it was performed by the Woman's Symphony Orchestra of Chicago, a well-regarded orchestra of more than 100 musicians, with a full concert season and regular radio broadcasts. The women players could participate in rehearsals and concerts without threat to their personal safety or propriety, and the orchestra had sufficient funds and renown to invite Carrie Jacobs-Bond to speak on the theme of "women and music" in the 1934 concert featuring Price's concerto. The concert program was comprised entirely of work by women, and the performance aired over two radio broadcasts. This was a triumph for Price, coming a year after her Symphony in E minor was performed by the all-male, all-white Chicago Symphony Orchestra, and many identify this moment as the apex of her success.

Marian Anderson and the Lincoln Memorial Concert

African-American ethnomusicologist Alisha Lola Jones, by contrast, is "inclined to move away from proving Price's proximity to Great White Male Composers as her life's goal and career highlight," and a feminist instructor can focus instead on Marian Anderson's performance of "My Soul's Been Anchored in the Lord" in her legendary recital at the Lincoln Memorial.[19] Jones observes that Price was the only composer identified by first and last name in the printed program for Anderson's recital, proclaiming her gender without compromise. What's more, Price's arrangement of the spiritual was the closing piece in the program. Anderson thus used her considerable clout to introduce Price to an immense and important audience, and "My Soul's Been Anchored in the Lord" became a signature piece for the singer.

The story of Anderson's concert at the Lincoln Memorial involves white women working for and against the artist, as is probably well known. The singer was denied permission to perform in Washington's Constitution Hall by a genteel ladies' group called The Daughters of the American Revolution, who owned the venue. Women seeking to join the DAR must prove their direct descent from an ancestor involved in the US Revolution, so membership is *de facto* restricted to white women, and Anderson was disallowed from performing in their hall even though the city's segregation policies were less rigid. Anderson moved her program to the Washington Mall at the invitation of Howard University, and with the approval of Eleanor Roosevelt, whose role as white savior has tended to be aggrandized. Regardless, the Lincoln Memorial concert was a triumph for Marian Anderson, and, symbolically, for all Black women. It was a glorious repudiation of the white supremacist gatekeepers of Washington's music community, particularly the unsisterly Daughters of the American Revolution. Through addressing the role of DAR in Anderson's career—and, by extension, in Price's—an instructor can acknowledge the nuances of feminist solidarity and show that women's activism is not always in support of all women.

Through her championing of Price's work, Anderson positioned herself as an influencer and connoisseur of new music, which certainly enhanced her renown as an artist. The singer and the composer met in Chicago through the National Association of Negro Musicians (NANM). Thus, the story of Price and Anderson can lead to consideration of how clubs and volunteer groups operate in music communities. And since this kind of volunteer work is overwhelmingly carried out by women, this part of the lesson can help us to see women quietly making things happen behind the scenes. African-American musicologist Rae Linda Brown has asserted that "It was through NANM—and by extension the *Chicago Defender*—that Price's name was kept before the public for the twenty-five years she resided in Chicago."[20] Price's career would not have been possible without the loyalty and generosity of women like Estelle and Margaret Bonds, Marian Anderson, and the women in the NANM who hosted meetings, organized concerts, and wrote letters to the newspaper. Recognition of this work's importance can correct a distorted view of composers as individual geniuses who rose to success solely on the basis of merit.

Reflections and Connections: Women's Musical Networks in Other Regions

Price and her network of women are far from an isolated case in music history. Remaining mindful of Kim TallBear's admonition to celebrate relations to community and to the land, I encourage you to draw on the stories of your own region in teaching whenever appropriate, so that university graduates feel connected to the specific cultures and histories of the places they spend four years. In my case, it is easy to link Price, Anderson, and the Bonds women to the story of Portia White. White was a Halifax-raised singer, contemporary with Margaret Bonds, a contralto with a concert career that earned her the moniker "Canada's Marian Anderson." Presenting her story alongside Price allows me to teach my students that Nova Scotia is home to Canada's oldest Black community, still vibrant and distinct in the region. White's family history even presents a mirror image of the Daughters of the American Revolution, in that her mother's family roots go back to the Black Loyalists who came to Nova Scotia during the US Revolution, promised freedom and land by British colonizers then in power here (the story of this community is told in a well-regarded novel by Lawrence Hill, 2007's *The Book of Negroes*).

Like the Bonds women, White and her family were active in their church as musicians, and this experience honed White's performance skills and allowed her to cultivate a loyal following. Beyond the church, White benefited from the patronage and support of an organization called the Halifax Ladies Musical Club, which met regularly for concerts, lectures, and conversation, and which also donated books, scores, and prizes to support music education in local schools. In the late 1930s, when Portia White's talent indicated a need for training beyond what Halifax could offer, the Ladies Club raised funds to support her study in Toronto and, eventually, a concert debut at New York's Town Hall in 1944. The club still exists.

White and Price are examples of women whose careers were made possible because of the work of women, operating within the constraints of middle-class respectability and sexist, racist institutions of power. After Price's death, her daughter devoted her energies to preserving her mother's legacy, but for many years, Florence Price fit awkwardly within stereotypes of composers *and* conventions of Black women musicians—she was neither a blues singer nor an eccentric white man. Consideration of her context and career can illuminate the processes and networks that support all musicians, and it can correct the distortions of reductive histories of music.

Sample Lesson Four

Womyn's Music Networks

A lesson focusing on the women's music movement that flourished from the 1970s to the mid-1980s, with independent record labels and women-only festivals, presents an opportunity to examine a music community that was deliberately constructed around a specific gender and sexual orientation. This topic must be handled with the utmost sensitivity, however; one inheritance of this lesbian separatist society is the trans exclusionary rhetoric that continues to inflict great harm on trans and non-binary people and the people who care about them. Studying the history of this philosophy is valuable because it affords insight into how a doctrine of hate and exclusion can be embraced, even by people who see themselves as progressive and well-intentioned.

Maxine Feldman, Alix Dobkin, and the Birth of Women's Music

In 1969, a few weeks before the Stonewall Inn uprising that is heralded as the beginning of the Gay Rights Movement, US singer-songwriter Maxine Feldman (1945–2007) performed her "Angry Atthis" in Los Angeles. Feldman, who described herself as "a big, loud, Jewish, butch lesbian," had been expelled from high school and subjected to psychiatric treatment and electro-shock therapy because of her sexuality, and had also been banned from performing in coffee houses because she attracted "the wrong crowd."[21] "Angry Atthis"—the title names one of Sappho's lovers, but also plays, of course, on the homonym of "angry at this"—was later recorded in 1979 for Feldman's only full-length album, *Closet Sale*.[22] It is a stirring performance. At first, Feldman's deep voice rings out over nimble 12-string guitar picking, with the words "I hate not being able to hold my lover's hand." As the tempo accelerates, her singing and playing become more raw and urgent, as she sings about wanting to stop living in fear and shouts that she is "no longer afraid to be a lesbian." "Angry Atthis," and the story of Feldman's personal suffering, will shock those students who may know little about the persecution of lesbians and gay men in the late 20th-century United States, but they should also find the song powerful and moving.

"Angry Atthis" is an important forerunner, but as a 24-year-old college student on strained terms with her family, Feldman had limited access to recording and distribution tools in 1969. She continued to be active as a musician, playing a central role in the Michigan Women's Music Festival (founded in 1975) until her death in 2007. The first full-length album of what would come to be called "women's music" is acknowledged to be 1973's *Lavender Jane Loves Women,* recorded in New York by Alix Dobkin (1940–2021). Dobkin, who had been raised by Jewish intellectuals and activists in Philadelphia, was involved in the politically engaged folk music scene of the 1960s. As a folk singer, she shared space with the likes of Bob Dylan, and she married the manager of Greenwich Village's Gaslight Café before falling in love with a woman and embracing lesbianism as her life's cause. With a vision of lesbian communities and women-only utopias, Dobkin dedicated herself to performing music for women, and she was able to draw on skills and contacts she had made on the folk music circuit.

She organized an all-female music production and engineering team to produce her record, founding the label Women's Wax Works and selling copies of the album through ads in *Ms.* magazine, *Off Our Backs*, and other feminist publications. It has been described as

> Revolutionary ... it was an out lesbian album, made by, for and about lesbians. Never done before. It was empowering on many levels. For one thing, the record industry at that time was closed to women except for female singers. The idea that lesbians made this album themselves was astounding. There weren't even any women record distributors yet. And of course, the music was good, fun and in your face. It was part of the creation of women's music and it announced something national and powerful about lesbian culture.[23]

It is hard to overstate the significance of this achievement, and we should note that the album's 1973 release predates disco anthems embraced by the queer community, like Gloria Gaynor's "I Will Survive" (1977) or Sylvester's "You Make Me Feel (Mighty Real)" (1978). *Lavender Jane Loves Women* is the first—by a considerable margin—openly gay, full-length record to circulate commercially.

The material on the album is built around Dobkin's warm, unaffected vocals and acoustic guitar. It features flute, acoustic bass, and classical strings (notably, no percussion), in verse-chorus songs with titles such as "The Woman in Your Life is You," and "Talking Lesbian." Students will almost certainly struggle with the ham-fisted musicianship and with the record's overall earnestness; the esthetic is different from the raw anger of Maxine Feldman, and strongly reminiscent of the 1960s folk scene from which Dobkin emerged. It will be helpful to reassure first-time listeners that many of the songs are intended to be funny, and that it's ok to giggle at "View from Gay Head," with its pseudo-Baroque flute phrases, enthusiastic, amateurish choir, and cheerful exhortation that "it's a pleasure to be a lesbian."[24]

At the same time, students must be prepared for the fact that the song articulates a freedom for lesbians that is firmly rooted in a binary notion of gender, with lyrics like "One or the other a person must be, the men are they, the women are we." The chorus implies that lesbianism is a choice, reinforcing the contemporary view that same sex relationships were "a political imperative" for feminists.[25] This rhetoric may have been liberating to many, but it goes against recognizing sexuality as fundamental to identity. As an emblem of what would be called "women's music," the song and the album were groundbreaking in their unabashed celebration of lesbian lives, but the commitment to "women born women" that became entrenched in the women's music scene is distressing, to say the least.

In teaching about this network and its goals of using music to resist heteronormative patriarchal oppression, then, it is important to stress that the desire for women-only spaces was problematic from the very start. Indeed, when we note that Maxine Feldman sometimes used male pronouns toward the end of his/her life, but told friends s/he was too old for the sex reassignment surgery that was by then becoming easier to access, it becomes possible to see that doctrinaire, trans-exclusionary rhetoric was never shared by all in the women's music community.[26]

Music and Lesbian Utopias

Lavender Jane Loves Women inspired further efforts to build lesbian community around music, and several women-only institutions developed through the 1970s, including record labels, concert tours, and music festivals, to say nothing of women's marches and other community-building events that did not revolve around music. In Washington DC, a group of queer women led by Judy Dlugacz formed Olivia Records and released their first album in 1974, Meg Christian's *I Know You Know*, which includes "Song to my Mama" and the wryly humorous "Ode to a Gym Teacher." The label moved to California the next year, and released Cris Williamson's *Changer and the Changed* in 1975, and this album would become one of the top-selling releases by any independent record label.[27]

Williamson (b. 1947), a white woman raised in Deadwood, South Dakota, was a considerably more sophisticated musician than Christian, Dobkin, or Feldman; a seasoned performer and writer, she had recorded her first album of original songs at the age of 16. The performer credits for *Changer and the Changed* alone indicate an ambitious scope, with Williamson herself playing piano, Fender Rhodes, and guitar on tracks that include fretless bass, percussion, classical strings, flute, banjo, and synthesizer. "Hurts Like the Devil" skillfully deploys an upbeat country groove (with banjo, and solo guitar from June Millington) to offset the anguished lyrics about heartbreak, and the beautiful "Waterfall" uses inventive phrasing and harmonies to create a contemplative mood that builds to an anthemic end, with Williamson's voice soaring joyfully over a chorus of singers.

The record production is also more polished than was the case with *Lavender Jane Loves Women*, and the album was an excellent showcase for the skills of Olivia Records' all-female, all-queer team. It would be hard to overstate the value of this achievement, in a time when the notion of "women's lib" was controversial, when wearing pants could expose a woman to hostility, and when right-wing activists such as white Americans Phyllis Schlafly and Anita Bryant were building careers out of insisting that women should be able to find complete fulfilment serving as wives and mothers. Aspiring female sound engineers and record producers struggled to find work or learning opportunities in the established music industry, and so the Olivia Records collective made it a strategic priority to support women in perfecting their craft. The determination and cooperative spirit required to make a success of Olivia Records were nothing short of audacious, and their vision extended to working toward racial equity. African-American artist Linda Tillery joined the collective in 1975, contributing as a producer, background singer, and drummer, and later noted that "I'd seen the racism in the industry, but I liked working for Olivia ... Judy [Dlugacz] was inviting women of colour into what was then a very white collective. I discovered a lot of straight white women were listening to my music."[28]

Alongside the artistic and commercial successes of Olivia Records, then, we can recognize their achievement in creating space for community and collaboration. In a historical moment that regarded queer women with revulsion and rage, that condemned professional ambition in all women, and that was steeped in racist prejudice, their efforts to build sisterhood should be recognized as courageous. Olivia Records forged networks that allowed lesbians to work creatively together, sharing ideas, whittling techniques, and serving as interlocutors for one another, while being able to let go of the self-surveillance and constraint that regulated their experience in the general public. To be an artist, to create, and to collaborate with integrity and honesty, requires openness and vulnerability; it is scarcely possible to do this work while preoccupied with policing one's own behavior. The possibility of sharing the company of trusted friends, free to drop one's armor and concentrate on creative self-expression, was the true gift of the women's music scene.

The Michigan Women's Music Festival

Music was recognized as a means to bring women together and provide focus for community-building. In 1975, this vision led sisters Lisa and Kristie Vogel to establish the annual Michigan Women's Music Festival, which would become the largest and best-known festival of women's music, and would feature Williamson, Christian, Dobkin, Tillery, and Feldman—among many others—as performers over four decades.

The weeklong experience of camping, games, rituals, music, and workshops on topics such as masturbation, was offered to women in rural Michigan; attendees were expected to take shifts in preparing meals, offering childcare, and other tasks necessary to sustain community in a temporary village that would be built new each summer by an all-female crew. At its height in the early 1980s, "Michfest" attracted 8,000 participants each year to the mission of building community and caring relationships that excluded men and sexist constraints. Mothers were encouraged to bring their children, but boys over the age of five were restricted to a specific area of the camp. In this annual gathering that banned males from the land, women felt able to sleep outside, to shower in the open air, and to feel truly safe from harassment, objectification, and the threat of gender-based violence.

In their endeavor to create a space for women to be free, the festival organizers invoked Wiccan practices and legends of the Amazons, an all-female tribe of warriors who are described in Greek mythology; Maxine Feldman's song "Amazon Women, Rise" became the anthem that opened the festival each year. Ceremonies and rituals also borrowed freely from Indigenous cultures, with sweat lodges and sage burning, as well as non-Western cultural practices such as yoga and djembe drumming. This kind of cultural appropriation helped many festival-goers—the overwhelming majority of whom were white, educated, and middle-class—feel they were resisting the misogynist, oppressive values of Western, capitalist patriarchy and rediscovering a prelapsarian, matriarchal spirituality. Accordingly, many embraced the spellings of "womyn," "womon," and "womxn" as strategies to avoid embedding the word "men" in the term they used to refer to themselves. Along with their vision of women's community that could draw from cultures around the world and across history, the festival was committed to inclusion for disabled women, ensuring accessible spaces and sign language interpreters from the very beginning.[29]

Efforts to include non-white women were clumsier, however, for all that racial diversity of spiritual practice was celebrated. To be sure, Black performers were included from the first year, and Linda Tillery organized a gospel choir and a showcase of Black blues women that became regular features of the festival. Future stars of mainstream music such as Tracy Chapman and Sweet Honey in the Rock performed more than once. Still, non-white women reported incidents of casual racism, and in response, a Womyn of Color tent was established in 1989 to offer workshops that were closed to white women.[30]

The introduction of exclusive spaces for women of color was controversial, with some festival goers committed to an ideal of sisterhood that transcended racial difference. These insisted that women could not "experience any form of privilege, including racial privilege, due to societal misogyny."[31]

Reflections and Connections: The Emergence of TERF Rhetoric

This attitude could not withstand the recognition of intersectionality as a mode of being, but it was prevalent in the 1970s. The insistence that all women were equal under misogyny was, of course, a crucial impetus for the Combahee River Collective Statement's 1977 work to expose how race, sex, gender, and sexuality intertwine. But the most divisive controversy concerned the festival's adherence to the idea of "women-born women" and their adamant refusal to allow trans women in the festival grounds. To many, the sacredness of women's space was threatened by the presence of trans women, whose very bodies could trigger memories of sexual assault and other harms.

Furthermore, trans women and trans men were viewed with condescension for their willingness to rely on drugs and other tools of the medical industry to construct their identities. In a 2000 column entitled "Come Back, Little Butches," Alix Dobkin wrote about witnessing transgender presence at a "Creating Change" conference the previous year. Dobkin expressed concern that medically supported sex reassignment was "like tattooing, permanent body alteration, only more irrevocable, and it's quite the craze among young butches," and she went on to lament "their flight from womanhood."[32] Dobkin's sneering depiction of transgender identities as a betrayal of lesbian culture was denounced forcefully, but it was also clear that her disapproval was shared by many. In a 2013 letter to the festival community, responding to charges of transphobia and to a boycott in support of including trans women at the annual gathering, festival co-founder Lisa Vogel wrote that

> The Festival, for a single precious week, is intended for womyn who at birth were deemed female, who were raised as girls, and who identify as womyn. I believe that womyn-born womyn (WBW) is a lived experience that constitutes its own distinct gender identity [...] I reject the assertion that creating a time and place for WBW to gather is inherently transphobic. This is a false dichotomy and one that prevents progress and understanding.[33]

Vogel's defense of the policy was not well received by those advocating for greater inclusion, and the Michigan Women's Music Festival held its last gathering in 2015.

Many of your students will feel no compunction about the demise of this festival; they may understand it as quaint at best and hateful at worst. They may find it easier to celebrate the value of Lilith's Fair, a women-centric music festival which ran 1997–1999 and worked toward inclusion in its artist lineups, its open admission, and in the fact that it toured the USA (with some dates in Canada). Many of the artists who performed at Lilith's Fair were openly gay, an indication of cultural shifts between the 1970s and 1990s that were achieved, in part, through women's music and lesbian activism.

With care, we can encourage students to see the women's music network as a complex case study that requires nuanced approaches and resists any clear conclusions. The goal of creating spaces where women could feel safe and free to be themselves, allowing even those who had survived violence to relax their guard, can surely be recognized as positive—indeed, sex-segregation around the world continues to be a crucial strategy in protecting women and girls from male harassment and violence. At the same time, the rigid, rule-bound thinking that excludes trans women from women's spaces is toxic and harmful. The lessons here show that even well-intentioned, progressive thinkers can inflict harm. They teach us also that a lens considering intersectionality is an excellent tool for dismantling hierarchies of oppression. Through studying the women's music movement, warts and all, we can help students to see history as a messy, non-linear path that involves false starts and colossal blunders, rather than a clean, unambiguous account of good and bad. This lesson can be empowering to us today as we continue to make mistakes, pick ourselves up, and keep going in our work toward justice.

Discussion/Assignment Questions

1 Many salonnières were honored with dedications in published musical works, and this token of appreciation provides a clue to their importance. Ask your students to investigate the identity of a work's dedicatee, perhaps in a piece they have performed or otherwise feel a connection to. Who was this person, and what was her role in the composer's career? How did she live, and where did her money come from? What role did music play in her life?

2 In the 21st-century cultural economy, social media influencers wield quite a lot of power. Many female influencers earn an

impressive income from sharing their preferences in fashion, makeup, home décor, and "lifestyle" choices, and much of their work involves showcasing an image of idealized domesticity. Are "mommy influencers" the descendants of salonnières?
3 What musical clubs exist in your community, and how does gender function in these networks? Ask your students to investigate the history of a local club, considering what participation offered to its members in terms of identity formation and community building.
4 How do other music festivals forge identity, and how do attendees experience and navigate gender and sexuality at these festivals? How is community built through participation in festivals ranging from Tanglewood to Burning Man; who is excluded, and how are inclusion and exclusion understood by attendees?

Notes

1. Nancy Hartsock, "The Feminist Standpoint: Toward a Specifically Feminist Historical Materialism," in Carole McCann and Seung-Kyung Kim, eds., *The Feminist Theory Reader: Local and Global Perspectives* (New York: Routledge, 2003 [1983]), 292–307: 301.
2. *The Combahee River Collective Statement*. United States, 2015. Web Archive. https://www.loc.gov/item/lcwaN0028151/. The Combahee River Collective named themselves in honor of Harriet Tubman's most audacious raid; in 1863, Tubman led a military operation in South Carolina that emancipated approximately 800 enslaved Black people.
3. Sophie Fuller, "Elgar and the Salons: The Significance of a Private Musical World," in Byron Adams, ed., *Edward Elgar and His World* (Princeton: Princeton University Press, 2007), 223–47: 243.
4. Susan Harris, *The Cultural Work of the Late Nineteenth-Century Hostess* (New York: Palgrave MacMillan, 2002); vii–viii.
5. James Ross, "Music in the French Salon," in Richard Langham Smith and Caroline Potter, eds., *French Music Since Berlioz* (Aldershot: Ashgate, 2006), 91–116: 93.
6. Ross, "French Salon," 98.
7. Ross, "French Salon," 102.
8. James Deaville, "The Well-Mannered Auditor: Zones of Attention and the Imposition of Silence in the Salon of the Nineteenth Century," in Christian Thorau and Hansjakob Ziemer, eds., *The Oxford Handbook of Music Listening in the 19th and 20th Centuries* (New York: Oxford University Press, 2019): 55–76.
9. Marie Anne de Bovet, *Charles Gounod, His Life and His Works* (London: Sampson Low, Marston, Searle & Rivington, 1891): 81.
10. de Bovet, *Charles Gounod*, 180.
11. https://en.tchaikovsky-research.net/pages/Nadezhda_von_Meck, accessed November 13, 2021.
12. Edward Lockspeiser, "Debussy, Tchaikovsky, and Madame von Meck," *Musical Quarterly* 22/1 (January, 1936), 38–44: 38.

13. Lockspeiser, "Debussy, Tchaikovsky, and Madame von Meck," 42.
14. Edward Lockspeiser, for example, writes of von Meck's "strange passion" for Tchaikovsky "which she sublimated in the letters she incessantly wrote him over a period of sixteen years," and he omits even to mention that Tchaikovsky wrote to her! Lockspeiser, "Debussy, Tchaikovsky, and Madame von Meck," 39.
15. Ann Powers, *Good Booty: Love and Sex, Black and White, Body and Soul in American Music* (New York: HarperCollins, 2014), 214.
16. Norma Coates, "Teenyboppers, Groupies, and Other Grotesques: Girls and Women in Rock Culture in the 1960s and Early 1970s," *Journal of Popular Music Studies* 15/1 (June, 2003), 65–94: 84.
17. Gerrick D. Kennedy, "How a Homeless Songwriter's Story of Heartbreak Made it into Beyoncé's Album," *Los Angeles Times*, June 15, 2016. https://www.latimes.com/entertainment/music/la-et-ms-beyonce-sandcastles-berry-20160613-snap-htmlstory.html, accessed October 19, 2021.
18. Quoted in Rae Linda Brown, "Introduction" in Florence Price, *Symphonies Nos. 1 & 3*, eds. Rae Linda Brown and Wayne Shirley (Middleton, WI: A-R Editions, 2019), xxxi.
19. Alisha Lola Jones, "Lift Every Voice: Marian Anderson, Florence B. Price and the Sound of Black Sisterhood," NPR *Turning the Tables*, August 30, 2019.
20. Rae Linda Brown, "Introduction" in Florence Price, *Symphonies Nos. 1 & 3*, eds. Rae Linda Brown and Wayne Shirley (Middleton, WI: A-R Editions, 2019), xxxi.
21. Frank Cullen, with Florence Hackman and Donald MacNeilly, *Vaudeville Old & New: An Encyclopedia of Variety Performers in America, Volume 1* (New York: Routledge, 2007), 374.
22. https://www.youtube.com/watch?v=-ZwnYY2Yg78, accessed December 3, 2021
23. Boo Price, quoted in Chrissie Dickinson, "Dobkin a Light for Lesbians," *Chicago Tribune*, May 17, 2012. https://www.chicagotribune.com/entertainment/ct-xpm-2012-05-17-ct-ott-0518-alix-dobkin-2-20120517-story.html, accessed October 12, 2021.
24. Alix Dobkin, "View from Gay Head," *Lavender Jane Loves Women* https://www.youtube.com/watch?v=m-eUr4wTAic, accessed November 3, 2021.
25. Anne M. Valk, *Radical Sisters: Second-Wave Feminism and Black Liberation in Washington, D.C.* (Champaign: University of Illinois Press, 2008), 143.
26. Feldman's exploration of gender identity is described at https://jwa.org/weremember/feldman-maxine, accessed December 3, 2021.
27. Judith Peraino, *Listening to the Sirens: Musical Technologies of Queer Identity from Homer to Hedwig* (Berkeley: University of California Press, 2005), 169.
28. Linda Tillery, quoted in Andrew Male, "'Our Sound Engineer Got a Death Threat': How Lesbian Label Olivia Shook Up Music," *The Guardian*, July 19, 2020. https://www.theguardian.com/music/2020/jul/19/lesbian-record-label-olivia-linda-tillery-californian-feminists-death-threat-music, accessed December 14, 2021.

29. Elizabeth Currans, "Transgender Women Belong Here: Contested Feminist Visions at the Michigan Womyn's Music Festival," *Feminist Studies* 46/2 (2020), 459-88: 472–3.
30. Thistle Pettersen, "Amoja Rivers, Separatist Space, and MichFest," *Feminist Current*, May 11, 2016. https://www.feministcurrent.com/2016/05/11/amoja-threerivers-separatist-space-michfest, accessed November 4, 2021.
31. Currans, "Trans Women Belong Here," 472.
32. Alix Dobkin, "Come Back, Little Butches," *Windy City Times,* January 26, 2000. https://xxamazons.org/emperors-new-gender-part-2/, accessed November 4, 2021.
33. http://michfest.com/letter-to-the-community-4_11_13/, accessed December 5, 2021.

Further Reading

Powers, Ann. *Good Booty: Love and Sex, Black and White, Body and Soul in American Music*. New York: HarperCollins, 2014.

Thorau, Christian and Hansjakob Ziemer, eds., *The Oxford Handbook of Music Listening in the 19th and 20th Centuries*. New York: Oxford University Press, 2019.

Coates, Norma. "Teenyboppers, Groupies, and Other Grotesques: Girls and Women in Rock Culture in the 1960s and Early 1970s," *Journal of Popular Music Studies* 15/1 (Winter, 2003): 65–94.

Currans, Elizabeth. "Transgender Women Belong Here: Contested Feminist Visions at the Michigan Womyn's Music Festival," *Feminist Studies* 46/2 (Winter, 2020): 459–88.

Fuller Sophie., "Elgar and the Salons: The Significance of a Private Musical World." In *Edward Elgar and His World*, edited by Byron Adams, 223–47. Princeton: Princeton University Press, 2007.

Ross, James. "Music in the French Salon." In *French Music Since Berlioz*, edited by Richard Langham Smith and Caroline Potter, 91–116. Aldershot: Ashgate, 2006.

2 Composition

In efforts to create an inclusive history of music, an instructor's first instinct will be to add composers from equity-deserving groups to their syllabus. This is an important and valuable step toward inclusivity, and there are many resources to support that approach. In this module of my book, however, I don't seek to supplant the multiple lists of queer, female, and non-binary composers in genres from jazz to chant to musical theatre. Instead, I hope to illuminate how gender and sexuality shape the act of composing music, as well as how music shapes our shared notions of genders and sexualities.

By placing it as the *second* topic in a class on music, gender, and sexuality, I am already destabilizing composition's place at the top of the music hierarchy, as discussed in my Introduction. Even if you choose to begin your teaching here, I strongly encourage you to review the ideas and strategies presented in "Networks" before embarking on teaching about composition. That said: I do not oppose the study of composers! Indeed, I value close focus on a single composer and even a single piece of music, as noted in my Introduction. With a "slow teaching" approach and maxim of "an inch wide and a mile deep," you can lead your students to deep familiarity with a small number of compositions that may inspire them to explore further.

Suggested Topics

Here, I offer sample lessons as models of teaching gender in relation to a specific composer and work; a specific compositional practice; and compositional treatment of a specific theme. An examination of Berlioz's *Symphonie fantastique* offers a chance to teach about the language of wordless, orchestral music through the study of a work deemed a brilliant achievement of Romantic music. Because the symphony was created around an explicit story, or program, which trades on misogynist violence, this class topic permits an exploration of the attractions and dangers of toxic masculinity. By considering Blues Queens as composers, you can lead consideration of the sexist and Eurocentric assumptions that inform our stereotypes of a "composer." This topic will also correct the commonly distorted history of the blues by underscoring the Black women who were key to developing the genre, and who were among the first superstars of recorded music. The final sample lesson explores the theme of motherhood in the work of three songwriters: Joni Mitchell, Sinéad O'Connor, and Björk. This topic permits consideration of the policing of female sexuality and reproductive control, particularly the punitive attitudes toward unmarried mothers in the mid-20th century and the discomfort that continues around themes of pregnancy, miscarriage, abortion, and breastfeeding.

Sample Lesson Five

Symphonie Fantastique: Madness and Masculinity

For many students, particularly those who are non-majors and don't have a formal background in classical music, instrumental works can present significant barriers to understanding. For some of them, it will seem strange to think that orchestral music can tell a story. After all, there are no characters, no words, and no images to help them follow what's happening, and they may wonder how sounds by themselves can communicate ideas and information. Students who do have a formal background, on the other hand, will find it easy to focus on the notes, but they may struggle to hear past the technical aspects of melody, harmony, and structure to interpret what they hear as a form of storytelling.

Yet even wordless music has a text.

Musical gestures are freighted with associations with ideas, emotions, and people; the typical instruments of the orchestra, for instance, are strongly linked to conventions of gender (as are the typical instruments of a jazz band or a rock group, of course). In an early study of instrument choice in public school music programs in the United States, Harold Abeles and Susan Yank Porter found that primary-school-age children already had rigid ideas about instruments and gender, connecting drums with maleness and violins with femaleness.[1] In the professional orchestral world decades later, these associations continue to be legible; most of your students will agree that lower brass instruments and percussion are coded male, and that girls and women have to negotiate gendered expectations when they want to play. The notorious case of the Vienna Philharmonic Orchestra underscores the point; while they clung until 1997 to a policy of all-male membership because women on stage would distract from their focus, they made an exception when performing repertoire that required harp. Anna Lelkes, the harpist who would become the first woman to join the orchestra officially, had been playing with them for 26 years, on an *ad hoc* basis.[2] Among many insights to be drawn from this orchestra's grudging moves toward inclusivity, then, we can infer that the harp is so firmly coded female that this musical boys' club either couldn't find or wouldn't allow a male harpist to perform with them.

How Does Wordless Music Tell Stories?

So the study of a work composed for orchestra can be an excellent foray into discussing the ways that music communicates ideas about gender without using words. Whether they are music majors or not, university students have heard enough music in their lives to know—even unconsciously—the ways that certain sounds affect us as listeners. Your study of orchestral language and its constructions of gender can begin with encouraging students to recognize reductive clichés in music, by reminding them of the ways that an orchestral movie soundtrack communicates information about what is happening in the story. They already know that music tells us which characters are good and evil, when to feel happy, when to feel sad, when something scary is going to happen, when characters are falling in love, and more.

You might lead consideration of this idea using examples from one of the most famous film soundtracks of all time: John Williams's music for the 1977 film *Star Wars*. In the principal theme, Williams creates a sense of excitement and urgency, using brass fanfare in a bright major key, syncopation, short, staccato phrases, and upwardly thrusting melodic hook. This is music for a hero, and it tells us about determination in the face of obstacles, integrity, resilience, and eventual triumph. People watching the movie for the first time can hear this theme and feel confident that good will prevail in the end. Contrast this with the music created for Princess Leia's theme, where Williams uses woodwinds and solo French horn in a melancholy melody that never lands on its tonic and can't quite settle into its major tonality, evoking a wistful damsel who needs to be rescued and comforted. Of course, Leia turns out to be not that sort of princess! But Williams knew that this was the appropriate musical language to introduce the film's only significant female character (indeed, after the death of Luke's aunt, she seems to be the only woman in the universe) in a way that would ensure the audience's sympathy. Contrast this again with the music crafted for Darth Vader, the villain of the story, where the minor key, low brass, and insistent, militaristic march rhythm work together to sound ominous, menacing, and relentless.

Hector Berlioz: Madness, Music, and Misogyny

At the time of working on *Star Wars,* John Williams was already one of the most successful film composers of his generation, known for his skill in crafting melody and his expertise in orchestration. Williams had learned a great deal from studying canonical symphonic repertoire, including the music of Hector Berlioz, particularly his 1830 *Symphonie fantastique*. While many popular, accessible orchestral works in the standard repertory share this vocabulary of gendered musical language, I suggest that *Symphonie fantastique* is an ideal choice of study, not least because it is a programmatic work with identifiable characters and events. The story that the composer wanted his audience to follow along with as they listened offers a guide that students new to standalone orchestral music (i.e., not a soundtrack for a film or television story) will appreciate. Because Berlioz created this story himself and identified themes explicitly, the gendered aspects of his musical intentions are irrefutable. Students can learn to recognize the ways that Berlioz used specific sounds to communicate specific ideas, and they can apply these lessons to other orchestral and instrumental music.

One of the best features of this symphony presents a great challenge for teaching it. Its massive orchestration—more than 90 instruments are called for, including two harps that are used only in the second movement—means that live performances are uncommon outside major city centers. The work is so much more rewarding when we can see as well as hear it that I recommend assigning a filmed concert of the symphony rather than a studio recording, particularly if you are in a community where the opportunity to witness a high-standard orchestra in any concert is rare. The San Francisco Symphony Orchestra includes *Symphonie fantastique* in its excellent *Keeping Score* documentary series, and the relevant episode from 2020 offers a full performance of the entire hour-long, five-movement symphony, filmed in high definition and surround sound, that is exciting to watch.[3] The concert is preceded by a thoughtful documentary, narrated by music director and conductor Michael Tilson-Thomas, that offers information about Berlioz's life and introduces some of the significant melodies and other sounds that are part of the symphony. This will be enormously helpful to students who find orchestral music daunting, particularly those who are not literate in music notation.

The story of *Symphonie fantastique* is dark and troubling, above all in its presentation of violence against women. In the program that Berlioz wanted his audiences to have in their minds while they listened, the story is of a young, tortured artist destroyed by obsessive love. In the first movement, or scene, he dreams about his feminine ideal, then sees a beautiful girl just like his vision at a ball. In the next movement, he is enjoying a day in the countryside and daydreaming about what it would be like to be with her, when he begins to wonder if she might be unfaithful. Later, he takes opium and hallucinates about murdering his treacherous dream girl, and then he imagines being condemned as a murderer and executed by the guillotine. In the last movement, he imagines descending into hell and finding the girl there, but she has become a witch, so he watches her participate in a devilish orgy.

The story is a textbook depiction of obsession, paranoia, and murderous rage in response to sexual betrayal (whether real or imagined), and as such it affords insight into the workings of toxic masculinity. Within the logic of misogyny, women are to serve and support men, and their failure in this role is intolerable. At the same time, because men are socialized to conceal feelings of hurt and grief, the devastation of heartbreak can only manifest itself in rage. The protagonist of *Symphonie* becomes fixated on an idealized notion of the perfect woman, but his paranoia is such that he almost immediately imagines her betrayal and the pain her actions will cause him. Just as quickly, he sees himself punishing her with death, after which the story reveals that, far from the angel of his dreams, she was a witch all along.

Note that this horrifying tale never sees the protagonist interacting with his dream girl, and thus never having an opportunity to embrace her as fully and fallibly human. The only positions imaginable for her are of perfect virtue or irredeemable wickedness. Note also that the theme of murdering a woman as retribution for infidelity is pervasive to the point of banality; the Beatles' "Run for Your Life," Tom Jones's "Delilah," and Jimi Hendrix's rendition of the murder ballad "Hey Joe" are famous examples that spring easily to mind, to cite only recordings made in London in 1966–1967.

In Berlioz's case, it is quite clear that the *Symphonie fantastique* story was semi-autobiographical, as his memoir depicts an emotionally unstable man with a violent temper who once planned to murder three people in retribution for a broken romance. In 1830, Berlioz was briefly engaged to the Belgian piano virtuoso Camille Marie Moke, who broke off the relationship while he was studying in Rome so that she could marry piano manufacturer Ignace Pleyel. Berlioz planned a return to Paris to murder Moke, her mother, and her new husband before turning his gun on himself, and he acquired pistols, poison, and a dress with which to disguise himself as a lady's maid. He lost these items on the train and then was frustrated by officials at the French border; these delays gave him time to reconsider and abandon his plot. Recalling the episode in his memoirs, he wrote that "I was beside myself with passion, and shed tears from sheer rage; but I made up my mind on the spot what to do. My duty was clear. I must at once proceed to Paris, and kill two guilty women and an innocent man. After that, it would, of course, be incumbent on me to commit suicide."[4] A feminist reader alert to gender-based violence will be struck by Berlioz's conception of his romantic rival as an innocent man, while Camille's mother was as treacherous as her daughter. His logic, and his sense of self-importance, are consistent with the misogynist worldview that drives many abusers to kill women and those who help them when they attempt to flee the harmful relationship. A feminist lens in the study of Berlioz and his symphony can thus illuminate the twisted thinking that leads to gender-based violence and can teach awareness of dangerous signs.

Harriet Smithson, Obsession, and the Idée Fixe

Like his symphony's protagonist, Berlioz had come to Paris as a wide-eyed boy from a provincial town, throwing himself into the city's arts scene (despite his parents' expectations for him to study medicine like his father), and he became obsessed with a woman based on seeing her from afar. His muse for *Symphonie fantastique* was Harriet Smithson, an Irish actress who was playing the role of Ophelia in a landmark 1827 production of *Hamlet* at the Odéon Theatre. Smithson earned many fanatical admirers with her extraordinary portrayal of madness, which electrified French audiences even though most of them could not understand Shakespeare's language. Her performance made a tremendous impact on the Romantic art movement in Europe, as the distinguished US feminist literary critic Elaine Showalter outlines in a famous essay, "Representing Ophelia." Smithson's choices of costume included black dress, pale makeup, and bits of straw in her loose, unkempt hair, and her wild eyes and hushed voice depicted madness in ways that were both unsettling and alluring. This kind of acting was a dramatic departure from conventional performance technique, and Smithson's reimagined version of Ophelia inspired contemporary painters like Eugène Delacroix, who took a "strong romantic interest in the relation of female sexuality and insanity."[5] Toward the end of the century, Pre-Raphaelite painters such as John Everett Millais and John William Waterhouse depicted Ophelia frequently, and always according to Smithson's characterization (filtered through Delacroix). Arguably, then, Smithson invented the attributes of beautiful, macabre madness that would ultimately solidify into clichés of the Gothic.

Like other artists inspired by Smithson, Berlioz saw her performance dozens of times. He sent her feverish, confessional letters and rented an apartment near the theatre in order to watch her comings and goings, behavior which we can recognize as stalking. His obsession inspired the writing of his symphony, although it would be several years before they met and—somewhat incredibly—married. During the years in which she shunned his alarming passion for her, Berlioz invented meaning in Smithson's actions: musicologist Francesca Brittan notes that in his letters of the time, he called her "Ophelia" rather than "Harriet," indicating he was more fascinated by her theatrical role than by her true self.[6] Brittan understands Berlioz's fixation in the context of contemporaneous theories of madness and monomania, a psychological disorder described in an influential medical encyclopedia of 1819 as a fixation on a single idea.[7] Berlioz, who was, after all, the son of a doctor and had some medical training himself, was intrigued by the concept of monomania and adopted it into *Symphonie fantastique* as a musical theme that he termed "idée fixe."

This fixed idea representing the ideal woman appears in each of the symphony's five movements, in guises ranging from wistful and melancholy to depraved and cruel, as the protagonist's notion of her changes. In using a musical theme across several movements, Berlioz departs from standard approaches to instrumental music of the day, but he does adhere to custom by structuring his first movement around the scaffolding of sonata form. This convention was widely used in European music of the late 18th and early 19th centuries, as in Beethoven's Third Symphony, *Eroica*, of 1803; the structure requires two contrasting musical themes, typically a strong, "masculine" theme and a soft "feminine" one that is subordinate to the masculine theme. In other words, Berlioz's dark, misogynist fantasy was already going to be predicated on sexist logic for how music worked.

When it is first heard, the idée fixe is a gentle, dreamy phrase in the flute and strings that glides around the tonic and evades a clear sense of direction or key—in texture and affect, it is an obvious influence on Williams's Princess Leia theme. In its final iteration at the witches' sabbath, the theme has changed meter, instrumentation, and tempo, manifesting as a capering, braying sneer from the clarinet. In between these two moments, the symphony has explored soundscapes from pastoral to macabre, with a grotesque parody of the "Dies Irae" Catholic plainsong for the dead, the eerie sound of violins played with the backs of the bow, funereal bells, and a sonic depiction of a falling guillotine and the thud of a head into the basket.

Berlioz's letters and his sketches for the symphony indicate his fascination with madness, horror, and the supernatural, and his immersion into the Romantic Gothic movement well beyond the Parisian vogue for Shakespeare. In the years between seeing Harriet Smithson on the stage and completing the symphony inspired by his obsession with her, he struggled to establish himself in the city's serious music circles while also exploring the dark, thrilling ideas coalescing in art works such as Henry Fuseli's paintings like *The Nightmare* (1781), E.T.A. Hoffman's stories of fantastic horror in the 1810s, and Goethe's *Faust* (translated into French in 1828, and published with illustrations by Eugène Delacroix). Themes of madness and darkness were appealing before the Romantic movement, to be sure, and they endure in art and entertainment through the 20th century and into the present day. We may agree with Berlioz that wordless music is an excellent medium for exploring dark ideas and disturbing stories, because when we have only our ears to rely on, we are compelled to turn inwards to our own imagination and most secret fears.

It is surely significant that the protagonist of *Symphonie fantastique* is an anti-hero, and that Berlioz would choose to present himself as a villain in his own story. We can compare the story's protagonist with some of the famous anti-heroes of literature and film: the Joker from *Batman,* Hannibal Lecter, or Jekyll and Hyde, to name a few, are all fictional white men who fascinate because of their capacity for evil. What is the appeal and value of stories that invite us into the minds of monsters? When these stories are told well, listeners can find themselves sympathizing with the character, and this experience may inspire questions about the boundaries between good and evil. According to quantitative studies of film audiences, the principal audience for horror is young and male; they enjoy the adrenaline rush and excitement of witnessing terrifying acts, and they can also find that sharing horror leads to social bonding.[8] Contemplating dark characters capable of terrible cruelty—from a safe distance—appeals to young men pondering their own power as they come of age in patriarchal societies.

Reflections and Connections: Echoes of Music and Madness

Themes of malevolence and the macabre surface again in the music of young, working-class white men in de-industrializing Britain in the early 1970s, in the genre that would come to be known as heavy metal. The Birmingham band Black Sabbath used the sounds of down-tuned guitars, distortion, and howling vocals in songs like "Paranoid" and "Iron Man" (both 1970), which resonated with listeners unmoved by mainstream popular music. Here, as in lead singer Ozzy Osbourne's later solo work, frustrated young men could find a compelling guide through madness, alienation, and despair. For its fans, heavy metal music offered escape into fantasies of power, but also a language of rebellion and defiance. As US musicologist Robert Walser wrote in his pioneering study of the genre, "heavy metal's fascination with the dark side of life gives evidence of both dissatisfaction with dominant identities and institutions and an intense yearning for reconciliation with something more credible."[9] Musical expressions of gloom and horror serve a purpose, in the 1830s as now, in offering a forum and a vocabulary for young men forging their senses of masculinity. It is incumbent on music educators to understand the allure of this music, and its promise of power and charisma, so that we can help our students engage in it without losing themselves.

Sample Lesson Six

Blues Queens and Their Inheritors

In this lesson, the goal is to teach about a specific compositional practice, the blues, rather than a single composition. I place the blues here, rather than in my module on performance, partly in order to challenge the reductive, cliché image of a composer as a white man who writes notation. To recognize the blues as a compositional strategy—comparable to sonata form, perhaps—will in itself destabilize the pedestal for classical music in productive ways, and to celebrate queer Black women as composers will inspire curiosity about hierarchies in music creation. One of the most important questions we can address in teaching about composition and gender is: who gets to be called a composer? A thread on the magnificent Blues Queens of the 1920s can offer an important counternarrative to the conventional story of music composition in the 20th century.

Black feminist scholars in the United States have challenged feminist movements and anti-racist movements to serve the needs of women of color. The writings of bell hooks, Hazel Carby, Patricia Hill Collins, and Angela Davis (among others) raise awareness of the double burden assumed by non-white women in racist societies, and their work is an excellent starting point for the university instructor who seeks to learn anti-racist feminism. Historically, Black women in the United States have combatted racism, just as their menfolk have done; they have also struggled with sexism imposed on them from outside (as well as inside) communities that need to build up Black male authority and dignity.

Theorists of Black feminism celebrate the importance of fiction writers like Alice Walker, Toni Morrison, Audre Lorde, and Gloria Naylor for their inventive and beautiful use of language to expose structures of power. In an influential essay from 1987, Caribbean-US scholar Barbara Christian notes that

> People of color have always theorized—but in forms quite different from the Western form of abstract logic. And I am inclined to say that our theorizing (and I intentionally use the verb rather than the noun) is often in narrative forms, in the stories we create, in riddles and proverbs, in the play with language [...] And women, at least the women I grew up around, continuously speculated about the nature of life through pithy language that unmasked the power relations of their world.[10]

The recorded art of blues queens allows us to hear the literal and metaphorical voices of Black women, deploying personal experience, playful language, colorful imagery, and expressive performance. My premise, then, is that women of color have always composed—but in forms quite different from the Western form of abstract, notated composition.

The Blues as Compositional Practice

Most university students will have some familiarity with the notion of the blues, though it may be a romanticized idea of blues as a musical expression of deep sorrow that emerges instinctively and spontaneously from those who have "a right to sing the blues." In the broadest sense, this is true: the musical form of the blues developed among people enslaved in the Southern US, and it preserved some strategies from African music (flexible pitch, expressive timbres, and elastic time) while also absorbing European approaches to harmony and structure. Music that would come to be called blues, then, emerged from a place of collective trauma and festering grief. Yet the blues tradition includes musical expressions of great joy, and the blues harmonic progression can—and does—undergird the whole range of human emotion. This simple three-chord formula, connected to an AAB rhyme scheme in lyrics, is endlessly fertile and expansive, and its strictness has allowed for infinite play and improvisation; musicians who know the structure can create new material, through collective playing, in real time.

Although my history of blues begins with the first recorded blues compositions of the 1920s, I find it useful to open the lesson with Robert Johnson's 1937 "Crossroads." "Crossroads" is an extraordinary showcase for Johnson's brilliant musicianship and songwriting, and it also hands you a clear example of the blues formula and the ways that a solo musician can modify it for expressive purposes. Chances are high that some of your students will know this recording. They may at least be familiar with the story of Johnson, a singer/guitarist who recorded only two sessions before meeting a violent death, too soon for the New York music industry scouts who would venture down to Mississippi looking for him. Perhaps they have encountered the legend that Johnson sold his soul to the devil in exchange for unparalleled skill in guitar playing, and they may, like British blues revival guitarist Eric Clapton, regard Johnson as the purest and most authentic voice of "real" blues culture.

British journalist Dorian Lynskey writes thoughtfully about the erasure of women from the history of the blues, observing that leading thinkers of the era, such as Zora Neale Thurston, deplored the commercialization of a Black folklore tradition for the entertainment of white listeners. Lynskey notes also that white, male record collectors who began to codify a blues canon in the late 1940s "scorned the 1920s hits as commercial junk and sought out the obsolete flops that nobody else cared about ... [that] sounded like music from the margins, unloved and misunderstood."[11] In the 1960s, Clapton, like members of Led Zeppelin and the Rolling Stones, among others, would revere this version of blues realness, which suggested that authenticity was the prerogative of men.

So, it may be startling for some to learn that Johnson was not the originator of blues on record, that he probably perfected his guitar-playing through diligent practice rather than Faustian bargain, and that he was able to develop his style by studying recordings from the previous decade by the likes of Mamie Smith, Ma Rainey, Bessie Smith, Alberta Hunter, and Ethel Waters. To be sure, these women were themselves inheritors of an oral music legacy to which Johnson also had access, but their influence in shaping the blues tradition has been wrongly minimized.

Through the impact of the new, cutting-edge technologies of recording, blues women were able to be heard outside their immediate communities, and their voices set the standard that younger musicians like Johnson would follow. Daphne Duval Harrison's study of 1920s blues queens shows that singers who had previously made their living in nightclubs, traveling tent shows, and vaudeville were among the pioneers of music recording, and that the works they committed to vinyl became exemplars of blues music. Indeed, so successful were the recordings made by women such as Mamie Smith in the early 1920s that most record companies eagerly sought Black women to record, leading to a burst of artistic activity for singers who would claim the title of "Blues Queens."[12]

In many sessions, these artists would improvise songs to fit the time limit of recording, and their creation-in-real-time would be supported by instrumentalists who could follow, due to a shared familiarity with the blues' harmonic progression. Thus, as Susan McClary points out, "recording and its commercial and distributing networks did not merely preserve this music; it also actively shaped the blues as we know it."[13] The music left by stars such as Mamie Smith would come to be called classic blues; Smith's 1920 "Crazy Blues" was the first commercial recording by any African American singer, and its success helped to ensure the rise of "race records," a category of recordings aimed at a Black market.[14] Through the 1920s and 1930s, these records fed an appetite for larger-than-life Black women singers of the blues among white audiences in North America and beyond.

Bessie Smith, Empress of the Blues

The great star of this genre was Bessie Smith (1894–1937), the Tennessee-born daughter of a preacher who was orphaned at nine and raised in poverty by her siblings, but would come to be the highest paid African American artist of her day, known as "the Empress of the Blues."[15] Adored for her powerful voice, glamorous appearance, and defiantly rough-edged persona, Bessie Smith (no relation to Mamie) sang frankly about intimate relationships, the everyday difficulties faced by Black women in the United States, and a bold ambition for wealth and respect. In her personal experience, she encountered sexist expectations and resisted racist violence, as when—allegedly single-handedly, while the men in her band hung back—she chased off members of the Ku Klux Klan who were attempting to sabotage her performance in a tent traveling show in Concord, North Carolina in 1937.[16]

Smith's skill with pitch inflection, phrasing, and timbral variety set a standard for future singers of jazz, gospel, and blues music, including

Billie Holiday, Mahalia Jackson, Nina Simone, and Janis Joplin (who, famously, purchased a headstone for Smith's unmarked grave in 1970). In her compositions like "You've Been a Good Ole Wagon" (recorded 1925), "Young Woman's Blues" (1926), and "Dirty No-Gooder Blues" (1929), she presented an earthy sexuality and expressed her own desires in straightforward terms, only half a century after Emancipation and the end of legal slavery in the United States. In these recordings, she is accompanied by many of the best jazz musicians of the age, including Louis Armstrong, Fletcher Henderson, Charlie Green, and James P. Johnson, and the songs follow a pattern of call and response between singer and instrumentalist. The effect is of a dialogue, in which the instruments comment, often humorously and even salaciously, on the singer's declarations.

For clarity of recording, "Young Woman's Blues" is easier to listen to than "You've Been a Good Ole Wagon," for all that the latter features Louis Armstrong in its impressive five-piece ensemble. In "Wagon," Smith dismisses a lover who has become tiresome, while "Young Woman's Blues" asserts her rights to independence and "plenty [of] men," as she sings "I'm a young woman and I ain't done running round." In this song's lyrics, she explicitly rejects marriage, celebrates her "killer" dark skin, and brags about drinking moonshine, yet also describes herself as a good woman. This is an audacious boast in the context of the rigid racism and sexism of the day, and it signals the glorious defiance that Smith's fans loved. Supported by Fletcher Henderson on piano, cornetist Joe Smith and clarinetist Buster Bailey take turns responding to Smith's sung phrases, often with word-painting that expresses approval for her statements. The rhythm and phrasing are steady, standardized so that all musicians can improvise over a reliable pattern; this is the most striking difference between blues records by ensembles and by soloists like Robert Johnson, who could improvise more freely since he controlled all aspects of the music making. The song arrangement is sophisticated, featuring moments where instrumentalists drop out entirely for a few beats, both to create a stop-start experience for dancers and also to ensure that specific lyrics are heard clearly. "Young Woman's Blues" is an excellent example of Bessie Smith's artistry as a performer and composer.

Many of Smith's most iconic recordings are of songs where she is not credited as a songwriter; the question of authorship, always vexed in recorded music, is particularly murky in the context of blues music featuring Black performers in the early days of the recording industry. Some artists were so keen to record—and be paid for recording—that they surrendered their songwriting credit, and many record producers were canny enough to insert their names and ensure they would earn any royalties. At the same time, an artist with clout could occasionally bestow a writing credit to a friend in need of assistance. And while Smith's 1928 record "Empty Bed Blues" is credited solely to J.C. Johnson, a pianist who played with several bands in Chicago during the 1920s, it is hard not to consider Bessie Smith the author of this performance.

In "Empty Bed Blues," Smith sings the praises of a lover with a series of ingenious metaphors for his sexual prowess; he is a superb coffee grinder, he is a deep-sea diver who can touch the bottom, he boils her cabbage and overflows the pot, all while trombonist Charlie Green growls and whoops in response. This playful language is less explicit than the hokum blues style espoused by singers like Smith's peer Lucille Bogan (1897–1948), whose raunchy 1935 recording "Shave 'Em Dry" is too frank for most classrooms, and it aligns with the practice of "Signifying." As theorized by African American scholar Henry Louis Gates in 1988, Signifying is a form of wordplay that trades on hidden meanings and teasing delivery to communicate meaning to those who have inside knowledge, such as using insulting language to show affection for a friend.[17] In the context of talking about sex, Signifying uses wordplay and metaphor in order to be barely respectable, able to accuse critics of being dirty-minded if they challenge the literal meaning. This language (of lyrics and music) would become a crucial aspect of blues recordings.

Ma Rainey and Outspoken Queerness

In childhood, Bessie Smith began performing with her brother as a way to earn money, and she eventually joined a traveling troupe as a dancer, where she encountered a mentor in established singing star Gertrude "Ma" Rainey (1882 or 1886–1939). Rainey, born Gertrude Pridgett in the rural Southern United States (there is some uncertainty about the precise year and place), made her living as a performer before retiring from the stage and purchasing theaters in Georgia. In the last years of her singing career, she made nearly 100 recordings which afford a glimpse of her colossal talent. She was the first to record "See See Rider" in 1924, with her Georgia Jazz Band that included Louis Armstrong, Charlie Green, Buster Bailey, Fletcher Henderson, and Charlie Dixon (banjo). US blues historian Elijah Wald observes that "one of the eternal mysteries of blues history is whether her version was adapted from a song that was already wide-spread in oral tradition, or whether her record was so popular and catchy that it spawned the vast range of rural, orally transmitted versions that have been recorded since."[18] Rainey would claim to be the person who discovered the blues (a boast also made by W.C. Handy), and her performance style drew on vaudeville, minstrelsy, Black folk singing, and dazzling glamor.

Although it is among her last recordings, Rainey's composition "Prove It On Me Blues," recorded in 1928, provides a wonderful introduction to her work. Importantly, it demonstrates her unapologetic declaration of bisexuality with lyrics such as "Folks say I'm crooked, I don't know where she took it, I want the whole world to know." The record was advertised with a full-page ad in the *Chicago Defender*, with an illustration of the singer dressed in a masculine jacket, tie, and hat, flirting with two fashionable young women while a male police officer looks on.[19] The recorded performance features Rainey's deep, full-throated singing in dialogue with a trio playing banjo, washboard, and jug, these latter sounds created by ordinary household items in the resourceful approach typical of folk music and country blues.[20] In this and her mournful "Deep Moaning Blues" of the same year, Rainey and her band were inventive in creating soundscapes for her songs.

"Prove It On Me Blues" may have been inspired by a 1925 event in Chicago, when Rainey was caught having sex with female dancers from her show and arrested, to be bailed out of jail by her mentee and sometimes lover Bessie Smith.[21] Outspoken queer living was easier in the scandalous blues community than in mainstream, respectable Black society. Likewise, the Jazz Age nightclub scene during Prohibition years was already a *demimonde* so far outside the law that lesbians and gay men could express themselves with some freedom. In communities such as Harlem, a network of speakeasies, ballrooms theaters, and nightclubs formed a vibrant music scene that included drag balls whose popularity would extend to white tourists from Manhattan, part of a "pansy craze" that encouraged queer men to be publicly visible.[22]

Gladys Bentley, Harlem, and the Pansy Craze

In this climate of creativity, risk taking, and boundary crossing, blues singer/pianist Gladys Bentley (1907–1960), clad in a white tuxedo and top hat, performed risqué parodies of popular (white) songs as well as original compositions about proudly loving women. Bentley is among the artists depicted by African American illustrator Elmer Simms Campbell in a cartoon map of Harlem's nightclubs for the *New Yorker* in 1932, and she was described by poet Langston Hughes as "an amazing exhibition of musical energy—a large, dark, masculine lady, whose feet pounded the floor while her fingers pounded the keyboard—a perfect piece of African sculpture, animated by her own rhythm."[23] In recordings such as 1929's "How Much Can I Stand?" Bentley is more circumspect, using male pronouns to refer to her overbearing lover, and the performance hews close to the standard blues format used by Smith, Rainey, and others. Significantly, Bentley is accompanied solely by a guitarist, Eddie Lang, and she uses a vocal scatting style imitative of a trumpet to provide the "response" to her "call" in sung lyrics. Thus, even in a performance that is more staid and conventional than her outrageous stage act, Bentley takes the roles of both female singer and male instrumentalist.

At the height of her fame, Bentley was relentlessly provocative, flirting boldly with women in her audiences at venues like the Cotton Club, the gay speakeasy the Clam House, and the Ubangi Club (where she was backed by a chorus line of cross-dressed male dancers), and telling a gossip reporter that she had married a woman—a white woman, at that.[24] Sadly, the permissive atmosphere of Harlem during its Renaissance did not lead to permanent progress for queer folk across the United States and beyond, and in 1952, Bentley wrote an autobiographical piece for *Ebony* magazine entitled "I Am a Woman Again." Here, she described her joy and relief at being cured of her "strange affliction" by "the magic of modern medicine [which] made it possible for me to have treatment which helped change my life completely. I am happily married and living a normal existence."[25]

Bentley's article is vague about the specifics of her treatment; she mentions female hormone injections and alludes, with Freudian overtones, to the curative power of true love. This may generate some skepticism in a reader who is knowledgeable about medical practice. At the time, US Senator Joseph McCarthy was leading a right-wing backlash and hunt for communists and so-called "social deviants," and the United States House of Representatives Committee on Un-American Activities (HUAC) was empowered to investigate the possibility of deviance and subversion in the lives of private citizens. US historian James F. Wilson has suggested that Bentley's renunciation of her glorious queerness was a savvy maneuver of self-preservation and also a ploy to revive interest in her flagging career as she approached her 50s.[26] Having already outlived Ma Rainey and Bessie Smith by more than a decade, Bentley can scarcely be blamed if she resorted to strategies that seem antithetical to the Blues Queen playbook.

Reflections and Connections: Musical Heirs of the Blues Queens

Yet the frankness, playfulness, and impudence of the classic blues lived on, shape-shifting with the rise of rock'n'roll and new technologies of music-making. Willie Mae "Big Mama" Thornton (1926–1984) was an Alabama-born, big-voiced and big-bodied blues singer, who wore men's clothes on stage and was "a bridge figure between the blues women of the 1920s and the rhythm and blues women of the rock and roll era."[27] Thornton's 1952 recording of "Hound Dog" featured an electric guitar as a duet partner in the place of trombone, cornet, or jug, but her Signifying caricature of a lover snuffling haplessly at her ... *door* carried over into the most famous recording of the song, by straight, white rock'n'roller Elvis Presley (1935–1977).

Presley's peer "Little" Richard Penniman (1932–2020) was Black and queer, and sometimes claimed that if Elvis was the King of Rock'n'Roll, then he himself was the Queen. He experienced playing in gay clubs and drag shows in the 1940s and 50s, such as the one hosted by Black drag star Patsy Vidalia (aka Irving Ale, 1921–1982) at New Orleans's famous Dew Drop Inn. Little Richard himself performed occasionally in a drag persona called Princess Lavonne.[28] Even in his mainstream career, he was famed for a flamboyant stage presence that involved dramatic makeup and wigs, and highly energetic movement, and he always acknowledged the influence of fellow queer performers such as Eskew Reeder, whose quasi-operatic singing and pounding approach to the piano were influential models.[29] His rough-edged, powerful voice evoked the charisma of Bessie Smith or Gladys Bentley, and he memorialized drag communities in his 1970 blues "Dew Drop Inn."

Little Richard and Elvis Presley were architects of rock'n'roll, shaping youth culture for ensuing generations, so the blues became a central soundtrack to the experience of youth in the 20th century and beyond. The blues became, inarguably, the dominant form of musical expression in the 20th century, giving rise to new forms of popular music such as jazz, gospel, rock'n'roll, rock, rhythm & blues, and informing also many avant-garde and experimental musics. Through the central, mainstream presence of the blues, it is possible to see that the legacy of the Blues Queens lives to this day.

Sample Lesson Seven

Motherhood

The notion of the hero's quest is central to narrative art forms. Tolkien's *Lord of the Rings* story, George Lucas's *Star Wars* saga, and JK Rowling's *Harry Potter* series are among examples that adhere to the model Joseph Campbell famously identified as "monomyth." The phases of a hero's journey must include adventure, tests and trials, atonement, apotheosis, reward, and a road back, and this teleology is accepted as foundational to storytelling with universal appeal.[30] In principle, this "single great life-giving story that expresses itself in endless variations through the legendarium of every tribe and culture" can cast a female character in the hero's role.[31] Yet feminist critics have pointed out that the model of conflict and conquest is itself reductively male-oriented, not universal at all. Indeed, Campbell's archetype relegates women to the role of obstacle in a hero's struggle and overcoming, by identifying "woman as temptress" as one of the 17 phases of the hero's quest. True, the "temptation" may be adapted to a form that is not female just as the hero can be a woman, but a storyteller making these kinds of substitutions will still leave the structure of the hero's journey intact.

Birth: A Universal Theme?

The power of the hero's journey as the best (even the only) kind of story has impeded the reception of literary narratives that revolve around themes considered exclusive to women. Stories about birth, for example, are often considered to appeal only to mothers—even though all of us are born, while few of us will embark on a hero's quest! And when birth appears in a hero's journey, it is generally presented in ways that gloss over the messy realities of birth from the mother's point of view.

Literature and other art forms that centralize pregnancy, birth, and childrearing are conventionally relegated to women's stories, assumed to have limited interest for audiences more broadly. In music as well, themes of motherhood are rare, to the point that British musicologist Jennifer Barnes asks "where are the mothers in opera?" in an article that identifies a striking pattern of motherless heroines in operas of the standard repertory. Barnes suggests that to give an opera heroine a mother would reduce the author's opportunities to put her in peril; a girl who has a mother is more likely to be protected, taught, and advised on navigating the problems of an operatic plot, and thus less likely to need a hero. She also observes that "childbirth and aspects of motherhood are coveted and, yes, romanticized by the male artist" and that "the motherless opera heroine fulfills the needs of her spiritual father—she must rely forever entirely on him, and she will never grow up."[32] Yet real children are less docile, and the experience of having a child is life-changing and transcendent.

In this lesson, I offer examples of composers who have created music based on their experiences of motherhood, choosing work that examines the painful, messy, and sometimes heartbreaking aspects of pregnancy, birth, and mothering. The pregnant body is still often viewed as monstrous, and the act of birth as repulsive, yet the experience of birth is among the only truly universal events in human life. A study of musical meditations on birth and mothering can be instructive and insightful in dismantling the fear of pregnancy.

Joni Mitchell, "Little Green"

One of the most famous songs about motherhood achieved widespread fame while hiding its author's secret in plain sight. Joni Mitchell wrote "Little Green" about the wrenching experience of having a baby girl and surrendering her to adoption, and the narrative song, written in the second person, appeared on her iconic 1971 album *Blue*. For decades, listeners failed to realize the song was autobiographical. The true meaning of the song's detailed, stark account became suddenly clear in 1997, when news broke that Mitchell had reunited with a daughter, Kilauren Gibb, born as Kelly Dale Anderson in Toronto in 1965.

Mitchell, born Joan Anderson in 1943, was raised as an only child in the Canadian prairie town of Saskatoon. When she became unexpectedly pregnant as an art college student in 1964, safe abortion procedures were not accessible. She traveled to Toronto, nominally to attend the annual Mariposa Folk Festival (where she did make her first significant performance), but also to hide her growing belly. In that city's burgeoning folk music scene, she began to build a reputation for her clear, bell-like singing, unconventional guitar playing (her hands had been affected by a case of polio in the Canadian epidemic of the 1950s, requiring her to invent her own chord shapes), and poetic lyrics. She told no one at home about her disgraceful, illegitimate pregnancy. Still, she yearned to keep the baby who was born in early 1965 when she herself was 21; that summer, she even made a hasty marriage to Chuck Mitchell, an older folk singer from the United States, in hopes of providing a respectable and stable family to her child. A year and a half later, however, she had moved to Detroit, given up the baby for adoption, left the ill-advised, toxic marriage, and embarked on her solo career.

During her early 20s in 1964–1967, then, Mitchell walked a gauntlet of shame, fear, and grief, which shattered her youthful dreams of an artist's life spent roaming the world and following her heart. She survived these ordeals and emerged as a brilliant, creative songwriter, albeit one with a secret that was unforgivable according to the social mores of the day.[33]

Mitchell became one of the artists whose name is almost synonymous with the singer-songwriter genre, a style of music typified by confessional lyrics, sparse instrumentation, and non-bombastic playing, recorded with transparent production values such as close microphone technique that fosters a sense of intimacy. This aesthetic dovetails nicely with notions of soft-spoken women in cozy, domestic space, sharing and inviting confidences, and building trust. Mitchell's work makes listeners feel not just that we know her, but that she knows us. In her songs, which came to set the standard for the confessional singer-songwriter genre, she left clues for her daughter, and in a later interview with Cameron Crowe, she revealed that "I started writing when I lost my daughter, and I stopped when she came back."[34] In her own estimation, then, the loss of baby Kelly was the impetus for her entire career; from her mother's grief was born a body of work that has been intensely moving and meaningful for generations of listeners, who had no real understanding of its inspiration.

Now that the story behind "Little Green" is public, it seems incredible that so many of Mitchell's critics and fans alike could blind themselves to the true meaning of this song, even while they admired her sincerity and soul-baring, confessional style. In a live performance at New York's Café Au Go Go in 1967, she actually sang her daughter's name: "Kelly green, be a gypsy dancer," and lyrics like "Child with a child pretending, weary of lies you are sending home" can scarcely be about anything *but* a secret, illegitimate baby.[35] Once she had achieved success and fame, there was near-constant speculation about which lover was the inspiration behind which song, so it is obvious that much of her work was received as an honest reflection on her real life. A song like "A Case of You" was pored over like a diary entry set to music, yet "Little Green" (from the same album) was commonly received as a poetic exercise in imagination.

This collective refusal to see what was in plain sight sprang, no doubt, from the fact that illegitimate pregnancy was an absolutely taboo topic in the mid-1960s. Upon reuniting with her daughter in 1997, Mitchell explained that "The main thing at the time was to conceal it. The scandal was so intense. A daughter could do nothing more disgraceful. It ruined you in a social sense. You have no idea what the stigma was. It was like you murdered somebody."[36] According to middle-class family values of the day, the shame of an out-of-wedlock baby could be the downfall of a family, which could even blight the prospects of other girls in the community. The idea of singing openly about it was unimaginable.

"Little Green" is a farewell benediction for Kelly, a loving way for Mitchell to send her forth into a new life with no expectation of seeing her again, since adoption records were closed by policy. Through the song's deceptively simple AABA structure, Mitchell's clear voice is heard in a melody of unexpected twists and turns, accompanied by her own guitar-playing, as she confers a happy childhood on the baby. Her lyrics refer to the seasons of the year as a means of marking the progress of time, a poetic strategy she would use also in "Urge for Going" (1965) and "The Circle Game" (1970). The effect is of a folk song; direct and intimate, yet also evoking the musical practices of another age.

Unwed Mothers and Magdalene Laundries

In "Little Green," Mitchell also sings of her struggle to make the right choice for her daughter. She addresses herself as "you" for a verse about signing the papers to release Kelly for adoption, metaphorically reaching back through time to comfort herself through that agonizing decision. Other work in her catalog reveals how this experience haunted her through the years: 1970's "The Circle Game" recounts a boy's happy childhood, but it can be heard as a fantasy of the life she hoped her daughter was leading. In 1994's "The Magdalene Laundries," some 30 years after her own pregnancy but prior to finding her daughter again, Mitchell takes on the persona of an Irish girl sent away to the nuns "for the way men looked at me." Here, Mitchell's voice has darkened and her lyrics are angrier and more blunt than in "Little Green," as she bitterly records the cruel irony of girls, many impregnated through rape, being forced to work in laundries "trying to get things white as snow, all of us woe-begotten-daughters in the streaming stains of the Magdalene laundries." Through this song, she is able to revisit and perhaps exorcise some of the shame and fear she was made to feel by the charity workers, nurses, doctors, and adoption agents she dealt with in 1965.

In a later interview with *The Irish Times*, Mitchell explained that this song was inspired by the grisly 1993 discovery of 155 unmarked graves on land belonging to the Catholic Church; Dublin's Sisters of Our Lady of Charity had been among many Irish institutions that incarcerated women and girls deemed "fallen," requiring them to work, unpaid, in laundries that brought profit to the church.[37] A few years later, English journalist Martin Sixsmith would work with Philomena Lee, a former inmate of Sean Ross Abbey, to seek the three-year-old boy she had been forced to surrender to adoption by an American couple who had come to Ireland in 1955 to get a new baby. Sixsmith and Lee discovered harrowing evidence of babies sold for profit against the wishes of their unwed mothers, who were obliged to work for the church unless they could pay to leave the asylum.[38]

Although the common assumption about the Magdalen asylums is that they were only for sex workers and unwed mothers, Mitchell is accurate in creating a character sent there simply because she was perceived as a temptation. As Irish historian Susannah Riordan explains, the Magdalen asylums of the nineteenth century were concerned with rehabilitating prostitutes, but they began, in the early 20th century, to incarcerate women as a pre-emptive measure. The cruelty visited upon the inmates has been disputed by many, who point to a lack of historical evidence that supports survivors' claims. Yet Riordan notes that it is impossible to know the full history because "archival records of women entering the Magdalen asylums after 1900 are closed to researchers by the responsible religious orders."[39]

As James Smith observes, the Catholic Church's continued secrecy and holding back of records mean that Magdalen laundries can only exist "at the level of story rather than history."[40] And story is often the best place to seek women's voices and histories. Songs like Mitchell's contribute to this particular story, as she lends her compositional talents to painting a vivid picture of lives thwarted by self-righteousness, hypocrisy, and misogyny. We can consider her song an example of women's theorizing, like women's blues and along the lines of Barbara Christian's dictum discussed above, a means by which women can assert their own truths and record their experiences even when the more formal avenues of history are closed to them. These stories have been further marginalized by an adherence to male-centered monomyth, meaning that we must labor to recover women's story and history.

"The Magdalene Laundries" was written before Mitchell had reconnected with her daughter, and she later recorded a different version in 1999 with traditional, all-male, Irish folk band The Chieftains for *Tears of Stone,* their album of songs (folk and otherwise) with women singers. To Mitchell's singing and guitar-playing, the Chieftains add Irish harp and pipes, penny whistle, and fiddle, musically embracing this Canadian woman's song as part of Ireland's cultural heritage.

Sinéad O'Connor and Lost Pregnancy

Elsewhere on the *Tears of Stone* album, the Chieftains support Sinéad O'Connor in the traditional Irish song "Factory Girl," creating a drone background for her to sing in the haunting, melismatic *sean-nós* style at which she excels. O'Connor (b. 1966) is of an age with Mitchell's daughter, and her career as a singer-songwriter unfolded in a very different climate to the 1960s' folk scene. In an interview with *The New York Times,* she reports that her meteoric rise to pop stardom derailed her ambition to be a "protest-singing punk," musing that "It seems to me that being a pop star is almost like being in a type of prison. You have to be a good girl."[41]

O'Connor is a mother to four living children, but she has also written unflinchingly about miscarriage and abortion. Her second album, 1990's *I Do Not Want What I Haven't Got,* includes "Three Babies," a promise to lost babies that they will always be with her. This song lacked the drama or virtuosity of her recording of Prince's "Nothing Compares 2 U" from the same album. It offered instead an intimate and heartbreaking lament about miscarriage, a much underacknowledged topic, for all that it is a widespread occurrence. The gently rocking triple time, narrow vocal range, and simple, repetitious melody allow O'Connor to sing simply and soothingly, in lullaby style.

In 1991, a time when abortion was still a crime in Irish law, she created "My Special Child," a searing apology to the baby she had chosen to abort, and she recorded it on a four-song EP to benefit the Red Cross. In an interview with *SPIN* magazine, she spoke candidly about the circumstances that led her to choose abortion, and the cover for that issue featured her photo and the headline "Exclusive: Sinéad O'Connor on her Child Abuse, Sex, Abortion, God, and Music," ensuring that the information was highly public. "My Special Child" expresses the bittersweet, complex feelings of a mother with a living child who decides she cannot parent another; in a spoken interlude, she addresses the baby directly, saying: "You were precious to me." The song is a breathtakingly courageous expression of a mother's love and care for a baby that was aborted, and it complicates easy assumptions about the experience of abortion.

By this time, she had a son (born when she was 21) who figures prominently in a great deal of her later work: he is named in several songs, and even contributes a song, "Am I a Human?" to her 1994 album *Universal Mother.* As this album's name suggests, the theme of motherhood came to preoccupy O'Connor as she matured and struggled to make sense of fame, family life, and her purpose as an artist.

In 2010, O'Connor re-recorded "This is to Mother You," originally presented on her 1997 EP *Gospel Oak*: this new version was made to raise funds for the New York-based charity GEMS (Girls' Educational and Mentoring Services) and to raise awareness of sex trafficking and sexual exploitation of girls and women. O'Connor sings the first verse herself, followed by guest singers Mary J. Blige, and then Martha B., herself a sex-trafficking survivor who had benefited from GEMS' resources. With a three-chord harmonic pattern and a melodic range of only one octave, the song sits easily in most singers' voices—unlike most of O'Connor's repertoire—and its simplicity and directness reinforce its message of unconditional love and comfort.

Björk and the Corporeality of Mothering

Like Mitchell and O'Connor, the Icelandic artist Björk (b. 1965) became a mother at the age of 21 just as her career began (she would have a second child 16 years later, with a different father). Björk's work is more experimental and boundary-blurring than either singer-songwriter, drawing on electronica, jazz, and modernist compositional techniques as often as punk, folk, and choral music styles. She has also collaborated with visual artists, filmmakers, and designers, creating an eclectic body of work that is unusually adventurous for someone who has achieved chart-topping hit songs. Raised in a family of artists who recognized and nurtured her talent, Björk has always had the security and confidence to take artistic risks and push against social expectations.

In her 2004 *Medúlla,* she reflects frequently on mothering, including embodied experiences such as breastfeeding, in an album of songs created almost entirely with mouth sounds such as grunts, gasps, mouth clicks, sighs, and panting. In "Oceania," written with poet Sjón Sigurdsson and originally commissioned by the International Olympic Committee for the Opening Ceremonies of the Athens Games, she sings against a soundscape created by the London Choir to claim the role of Mother Ocean addressing her children "since you left my wet embrace and crawled ashore." In her performance at the Olympic Games, she wore a diaphanous silk dress which floated and billowed like waves across the entire arena floor as she sang, engulfing athletes and officials in her embrace.[42] In "The Pleasure is All Mine," Björk collaborates with Inuk throat singer Tanya Tagaq, New York beatboxer/rapper Rahzel, and the Icelandic Choir, to create a gorgeous, otherworldly reflection on selflessness and giving, celebrating her body's capacity to nourish her baby. In "Mouth's Cradle," she partners again with this group to reflect on the sensual pleasures of mothering and breastfeeding, depicting her baby's mouth as a cozy place of comfort and restoration.[43]

Discussing the genesis of *Medúlla*, Björk explains that "Giving birth makes you extremely conscious and you realize that this is the only thing that matters. This primal force ... I wanted to do a vocal album and I wanted it to have a strong feeling of heart, blood, and meat. And at the same time, I wanted the lower half of the body to merge into the music."[44] The music on this album, then, is rooted in bodies and their functionality, and the reliance on sounds made by the body is connected to her exploration of mothering. Björk's rhapsodic notion of birth as "the only thing that matters" risks essentializing female bodies as mere vessels, an uncomfortable idea for many students seeking equity and inclusion, so this statement will require careful handling.

Reflections and Connections: Shifting Attitudes Toward Motherhood

Björk's matter-of-fact explicitness about the viscerality of birth and nursing is breathtaking to consider against the strictures and repressions facing Joni Mitchell's generation of mothers forty years before. Indeed, it was bold according to attitudes of 2004, when many Western cultures viewed breastfeeding as disgusting and best conducted in private. In 2005, American television journalist Barbara Walters complained about public breastfeeding, and many US states resisted allowing the nursing of babies in public.[45] In response, the "lactivist" movement was born, with groups of parents assembling for "nurse-ins" in shopping malls, restaurants, and other public spaces.

In the 2020s, taboos around motherhood's more intimate and embodied aspects seem to be dissolving, and internationally renowned British singer-songwriter Adele foregrounded motherhood in her fourth album, 2021's *30*, presenting recordings of conversation with her son alongside candid musical reflections on divorce and solo parenting. Halsey, a non-binary singer/songwriter from the USA, released their album *If I Can't Have Love, I Want Power* in the same year; the lead single, "I Am Not a Woman, I'm a God," addressed the artist's anguish with miscarriages and their anxious joy in carrying a pregnancy to term. The album's cover image showed Halsey and their baby posed as in a Renaissance painting of Madonna and child, bare-breasted and seated on a golden throne. Halsey and other artists continue the work of resisting attitudes that view mothers' work with revulsion, demonstrating that feminist activism—including art—can

Composition 63

provoke reflection and discussion, leading us away from prejudice and towards greater inclusivity and true support for families.

Discussion/Assignment Questions

1 The music of video games is often highly sophisticated, and integral to the success of a game. In games from *Final Fantasy* to *Fortnite*, a score that draws on symphonic musical language communicates information about characters and events. In what ways does the musical language of video games construct gender identities? And to what extent does video game music participate in supporting the safe exploration of danger and horror?

2 Before Emancipation, enslaved Black women were denied control over their sexuality and reproduction, so the Blues Queens of the 1920s were groundbreaking in asserting ownership of sexual desire. How can we position latter-day Black women performers such as Lil Kim, Nicki Minaj, Cardi B, and others into this history? What is gained when we trace a lineage from Ma Rainey to Lizzo or Megan thee Stallion? Is there a danger of playing into racist ideas when Black women are portrayed as sexually voracious?

3 While cross-dressing and drag performance have long existed in queer subcultures, the style achieved widespread fame and acceptance in the 21st century through mainstream television shows like *RuPaul's Drag Race*, a franchised competition with 13 seasons with its original host (to date), and nationalized versions in countries from Chile to Thailand. Music performance is an essential requirement for contestants, and a central aspect of drag shows more broadly: what kinds of music work best in this context, and why?

4 The theme of fatherhood is examined and celebrated by male artists including Stevie Wonder ("Isn't She Lovely," 1976), John Lennon ("Beautiful Boy," 1980), and Will Smith ("Just the Two of Us," 1998). However, many songs about fathers express ambivalence or anguish about the relationship of father and child, as in Harry Chapin's 1974 "Cat's in the Cradle" or the Temptations' 1972 "Papa Was a Rolling Stone." How has the role of a father been limited by sexist expectations, and how might new approaches to fathering change family life for the better?

5 Finnish composer Kaija Saariaho is among a small minority of female composers writing large-scale orchestral and operatic works. In her 2006 opera *Adriana Mater*, the plot sees a woman considering

abortion of a pregnancy brought about rape. Compare this operatic exploration of the politics of an unwanted pregnancy to Janáček's 1904 *Jenůfa*.

Notes

1. Harold Abeles and Susan Yank Porter, "The Sex-Stereotyping of Musical Instruments," *Journal of Research in Music Education* 26/2 (July 1978), 65–75.
2. Francesca Jackes, "All-White on the Night: Why Does the World-Famous Vienna Philharmonic Feature so Few Women and Ethnic Minorities?" *The Independent*, March 4, 2010. https://www.independent.co.uk/arts-entertainment/music/features/all-white-on-the-night-why-does-the-worldfamous-vienna-philharmonic-feature-so-few-women-and-ethnic-minorities-1915666.html, accessed December 4, 2020.
3. https://www.youtube.com/watch?v=wWi3xslzeEY, accessed December 19, 2021.
4. Hector Berlioz, translated and edited by David Cairns, *Memoirs of Hector Berlioz*.
5. Elaine Showalter, "Representing Ophelia: Women, Madness, and the Responsibilities of Feminist Criticism," in Geoffrey Hartman and Patricia Parker, eds., *Shakespeare and the Question of Theory* (New York, Routledge: 1985), 77–94: 83–4.
6. Francesca Brittan, "Berlioz and the Pathological Fantastic: Melancholy, Monomania, and the Romantic Autobiography," *19th-Century Music* 29/3 (2006), 211–39.
7. Brittan, "Berlioz and the Pathological Fantastic," 220–22.
8. Among others: Ron Tamborini and James Stiff, "Predictors of Horror Film Attendance and Appeal: An Analysis of the Audience for Frightening Films," *Communication Research* 14/4 (1987), 415–36.
9. Robert Walser. *Running with the Devil: Power, Gender, and Madness in Heavy Metal Music* (Middletown: Wesleyan University Press, 1993), xvii.
10. Barbara Christian, "The Race for Theory," *Cultural Critique,* Spring, 1987/6, 51–63: 52,
11. Dorian Lynksey, "The Forgotten Story of America's First Black Superstars," *BBC Culture*, https://www.bbc.com/culture/article/20210216-the-forgotten-story-of-americas-first-black-superstars, accessed December 28, 2021.
12. Daphne Duval Harrison, *Black Pearls: Blues Queens of the 1920s* (Rutgers University Press, 2000).
13. Susan McClary, "Thinking Blues," in *Conventional Wisdom: The Content of Musical Form* (Berkeley: University of California Press, 2000), 32–62: 37.
14. Maureen Mahon, "How Bessie Smith Influenced a Century of Popular Music," National Public Radio's *All Things Considered,* August 5, 2019. https://www.npr.org/2019/08/05/747738120/how-bessie-smith-influenced-a-century-of-popular-music, accessed December 27, 2021.
15. Mahon, "Bessie Smith."

16. Adam Thomas, "On a Blues Woman's Birthday," *Feminist Wire*, April 15, 2011, and elsewhere. https://thefeministwire.com/2011/04/on-a-blues-womans-birthday/, accessed December 28, 2021.
17. Henry Louis Gates, *The Signifying Monkey: A Theory of African-American Literary Criticism* (New York: Oxford University Press, 1988).
18. Elijah Wald, "See See Rider (Mississippi John Hurt and Others)," *Old Friends: A Songobiography* https://www.elijahwald.com/songblog/see-see-rider/, accessed December 28, 2021.
19. Angela Davis, *Blues Legacies and Black Feminism: Gertrude "Ma" Rainey, Bessie Smith, and Billie Holiday* (New York: Vintage Books, 1998): 49.
20. This restored 1930 newsreel clip shows how a jug can be played by blowing across the jug's mouth, creating an impudent, cheeky sound. https://www.youtube.com/watch?v=l0WciUNrdJ0, accessed December 28, 2021.
21. Sandra Lieb, *Mother of the Blues: A Study of Ma Rainey* (Boston: University of Massachusetts Press, 1981): 17.
22. George Chauncey, "Pansies on Parade: Prohibition and the Spectacle of the Pansy," *Gay New York: Gender, Urban Culture, and the Makings of the Gay Male World, 1890-1940* (New York: Basic Books, 1994): 301–30.
23. Langston Hughes, *The Big Sea: An Autobiography*, 2nd ed. (New York: Hill & Wang, 1993): 226.
24. Haleema Shah, "The Great Blues Singer Gladys Bentley Broke All the Rules," *Smithsonian Magazine*, March 14, 2019, https://www.smithsonianmag.com/smithsonian-institution/great-blues-singer-gladys-bentley-broke-rules-180971708/, accessed December 28, 2021.
25. Gladys Bentley, "I Am a Woman Again," *Ebony* VII/10, August 1952, 92–6: 94. Found online at https://queermusicheritage.com/bentley6.html, accessed December 28, 2021.
26. James F. Wilson, "In My Well of Loneliness: Gladys Bentley's Bulldykin' Blues," *Bulldaggers, Pansies, and Chocolate Babies: Performance, Race, and Sexuality in the Harlem Renaissance* (Ann Arbor: University of Michigan Press, 2010): 154–91.
27. Maureen Mahon, *Black Diamond Queens: African American Women and Rock and Roll* (Durham: Duke University Press, 2020): 30.
28. Charles White. *The Life and Times of Little Richard* (Omnibus Press, 2003): 22–5.
29. Ben Saunders, "The 1950s Queer Black Performers Who Inspired Little Richard," *The Conversation*, May 19, 2020. https://theconversation.com/the-1950s-queer-black-performers-who-inspired-little-richard-138658, accessed January 19, 2022.
30. Joseph Campbell, *The Hero with a Thousand Faces* (1949).
31. James Parker, "Joseph Campbell's Woman Problem," *The Atlantic*, September 2021. https://www.theatlantic.com/magazine/archive/2021/09/maria-tatar-heroine-1001-faces/619494/, accessed December 30, 2021.
32. Jennifer Barnes, "Where Are the Mothers in Opera?" in Sarah Cooper, ed., *Girls! Girls! Girls! Essays on Women and Music* (New York: New York University Press, 1996), 86–99: 87, 95.
33. For more on this period of Mitchell's career, see Adam Behan, "Joni Mitchell's Urges for Going, 1965–67: Coffeehouses, Counterculture and Care," *Journal of the Society for American Music* 17/1 (forthcoming).

34. Joni Mitchell, quoted in Cameron Crowe, liner notes to *Dreamland* (Los Angeles: Rhino Records, 2004) https://www.theuncool.com/journalism/joni-mitchell-dreamland/.
35. This performance of the song, three years before she recorded it for *Blue,* is fascinating on many levels. https://www.youtube.com/watch?v=QPZ6P7D3BIw, accessed January 1, 2022.
36. Joni Mitchell, quoted in Bill Higgins, "Both Sides at Last," *Los Angeles Times,* April 8, 1997. https://www.latimes.com/archives/la-xpm-1997-04-08-ls-46389-story.html, accessed January 1, 2022.
37. No author given, "Witness of Life," *The Irish Times,* February 26, 1999. https://www.irishtimes.com/culture/witness-of-life-1.156993, accessed January 1, 2022.
38. Martin Sixsmith, *The Lost Child of Philomena Lee* (London: Macmillan, 2009). This book provided the basis for Stephen Frears's 2013 film *Philomena,* starring Judi Dench and Steve Coogan.
39. Susannah Riordan, "Challenging Bad Nuns: Ireland's Magdalen Laundries," *The Irish Review (Cork)* 42 (Summer 2010), 120–27: 121.
40. James M. Smith, *Ireland's Magdalen Laundries and the Nation's Architecture of Containment* (Manchester: Manchester University Press, 2008): 138.
41. Sinéad O'Connor, quoted in Amanda Hess, "Sinéad O'Connor Remembers Things Differently," *The New York Times,* May 18, 2021. https://www.nytimes.com/2021/05/18/arts/music/sinead-oconnor-rememberings.html, accessed January 1, 2022.
42. https://www.youtube.com/watch?v=Canm7glYFgg, accessed January 3, 2022.
43. A detailed musical transcription and analysis of "Mouth's Cradle" is found in Victoria Malawey, "Musical Emergence in Björk's *Medúlla,*" *Journal of the Royal Musical Association* 136/1 (2011), 141–80.
44. Björk Guðmundsdóttir, quoted in Shana Goldin-Perschbacher, "Icelandic Nationalism, Difference Feminism, and Björk's Maternal Aesthetic," *Women and Music: A Journal of Gender and Culture* 18 (2014), 48–81: 61.
45. Goldin-Perschbacher, "Icelandic Nationalism," 67–8.

Further Reading

Chauncey, George. *Gay New York: Gender, Urban Culture, and the Makings of the Gay Male World, 1890-1940.* New York: Basic Books, 1994.
Christian, Barbara. "The Race for Theory," *Cultural Critique,* 14/1 (Spring, 1988): 51–63.
Duval Harrison, Daphne. *Black Pearls: Blues Queens of the 1920s.* New Brunswick, NJ: Rutgers University Press, 2000.
Mahon, Maureen. *Black Diamond Queens: African American Women and Rock and Roll.* Durham: Duke University Press, 2020.
McClary, Susan. "Thinking Blues." In *Conventional Wisdom: The Content of Musical Form,* 32–62. Berkeley: University of California Press, 2000.

Osborne, William. "Art is Just an Excuse: Gender Bias in International Orchestras," *IAWM Journal* 2/3 (Winter, 1996): 6–14.

Powers, Ann. *Good Booty: Love and Sex, Black and White, Body and Soul in American Music*. New York: Harper Collins, 2017.

Showalter, Elaine. "Representing Ophelia: Women, Madness, and the Responsibilities of Feminist Criticism." In *Shakespeare and the Question of Theory*, edited by Geoffrey Hartman and Patricia Parker, 77–94. New York: Routledge, 1985.

Wilson, James F. *Bulldaggers, Pansies, and Chocolate Babies: Performance, Race, and Sexuality in the Harlem Renaissance*. Ann Arbor: University of Michigan Press, 2010.

Zoladz, Lindsay. "Joni Mitchell: Fear of a Female Genius," *The Ringer* (October 16, 2017). https://www.theringer.com/music/2017/10/16/16476254/joni-mitchell-pop-music-canon.

3 Performance

Shakespeare writes in *As You Like It* that "all the world's a stage, and all the men and women merely players. They have their exits and their entrances, and one man in his time plays many parts." This observation encapsulates the notion that all public life is performance. In his 1959 *The Presentation of Self,* noted US sociologist Erving Goffman builds on it to argue that life is a series of performances through which we construct and manage our identities. To students living in an age of ubiquitous social media, this idea should be easily understandable and relatable. Through various social media platforms, people choose carefully which pictures and anecdotes to share, mindful of the story these items will tell. What's more, users of more than one platform may perform their identity quite differently for professional, peer, and family audiences. This is also true in everyday life, as we all play many roles in our families, our workplaces, our places of learning, and elsewhere. We use different posture, language, and affect when we speak to a grandparent compared to when we speak to a peer, and neither of these performances is dishonest: rather, our identities are complex and multi-faceted.

It's useful to help our students understand that we are all performing and creating our identities all the time, including our gender identities. Famously and influentially, Judith Butler has drawn on the thought of Simone de Beauvoir in order to argue that gender is "in no way a stable identity ... rather, it is an identity tenuously constituted in time—an identity instituted through a *stylized repetition of acts.*"[1] All of have been taught to train our bodies into compliance with socially accepted gender norms, through instructions to "walk like a man" or "sit up like a lady." We internalize these instructions to the point that our performances of our gender become automatic and feel natural. In a classroom, you can demonstrate the truth of this by asking your

DOI: 10.4324/9781003042655-4

students to notice their sitting posture at the moment and to reflect on its gendered meaning.

Some people choose performance as an avocation or career, and their approach will be more deliberate and mindful. Apart from singers, though, musicians rarely consider their performing work as comparable to acting. They may instead strive toward the best sound for the desired effect and see themselves more as technicians than storytellers. This attitude is often reinforced in musician training: as an undergraduate student majoring in voice, I was maddened that my performance exams involved assessment of my clothing, hair, and facial expressiveness, while my pianist roommate was graded solely on her execution of the notes.

Yet performance studies scholars such as Philip Auslander encourage us to recognize that instrumentalists also present musical personae while performing sound. He uses the example of "guitar face" to point out how instrumentalists are expected to express themselves through stance and gesture, even when there is no bearing on the sounds created. The facial gestures of a rock guitarist playing a solo "serve as coded displays that provide the audience with external evidence of the musician's ostensible internal state while playing."[2] In this way, all musicians use their faces and bodies to communicate hidden aspects of the performance and add layers to the storytelling. Sometimes, as with the example of "guitar face," the musician draws on dramatically expressive facial gestures to perform the passion and intensity felt, but the opposite can also be true. Consider the deadpan, stoic demeanor of John Entwhistle, bassist for British rock band The Who; his unperturbed cool in the midst of his bandmates' gleeful violence and onstage destruction of instruments was crucial to the band's appeal in the 1960s and 1970s.

In a module about performance and gender, you have the opportunity to explore the ways that musicians, and musical sounds, portray gender through many aspects of performance. What kinds of agency and authority does a performer have? Is it possible for performers to challenge the ways gender is represented and understood?

Suggested Topics

In the sample lessons in this module, I offer models for teaching about how musical performance can reinforce and also sometimes destabilize hegemonic gender norms. Through consideration of transgender voices, you can teach about fluid constructions of masculinity in opera and other vocal music. In a lesson on Tchaikovsky's *Swan Lake*, you can explore wordless musical portrayals of masculinity and femininity, and the ways in which dance and music work together to tell stories. With attention to Disney musicals created for children and their families, you can examine the ways that performance reinforces gender conventions but also resists them.

Sample Lesson Eight

Gender-bending Voices

In the opening paragraphs of his landmark *Cruising Utopia: The Then And There of Queer Futurity,* Cuban-American performance studies scholar José Muñoz writes that "queerness is that thing that lets us feel that this world is not enough, that indeed something is missing … Queerness is also a performative because it is not simply a being but a doing for the future."[3] This is, perhaps, nowhere more true than in the context of voices that trouble the gender binary, holding out the promise of something more in the future while making difference audible in the present. Understandings of gender and of queerness often inform one another, and there is much shared ground between queer identities and gender-bending ones—though it is a mistake to conflate these different ways of being. In this lesson, you can lead consideration of queer voices and how their performances insist on the complexity of gendered bodies, challenging us all to hear and speak thoughtfully. Through a history of singing that blurs rigid distinctions between biological sex roles, you can show your students how the human voice has been able to signal the possibilities of gender beyond the binary.

Castrati

In a music history class focused on gender and sexuality, a module on performance would be glaringly incomplete without consideration of castrati singers and their role in constructing Baroque masculinities. In teaching about castrato and travesti singers of the 18th and 19th centuries, however, it is important not to rely too much on our contemporary conceptions of gender and sex. These singers are sometimes compared to the "boy-actresses" of Shakespeare's day, as well as to drag performers of modern entertainment, but the circumstances and function of all these performers are specific and unique.[4] Your students will need careful support in their efforts to meet these performers in their own contexts and to consider the lessons they offer to us in our own present.

Performance 71

The castrato voice combined the range of a boy treble with the vocal stamina and lung capacity of an adult male, and it was achieved through surgical castration of boys before the onset of puberty. Students are invariably horrified and fascinated in equal measure when this topic is introduced, and it can be challenging to teach about castrati without squeamishness and crude humor. Yet because the Italian castrati were star performers who helped opera shift from an elite art form to a mass entertainment, studying their role in opera's development is central to understanding opera and bel canto singing more broadly. US musicologist Naomi André asserts that the sonic qualities of castrato singing present a kind of blueprint for bel canto technique and the heroic voice types (male and female) that became conventional in the19th-century opera.[5] Since the linking of high voices with heroism, nobility, and good character carried over into musical theatre singing as well, an examination of castrato and travesti singing can illuminate longstanding hegemonic ideals of voice types.

There are several reliable histories of castrati that provide accessible analysis without overdoing sensationalism, such as the hour-long BBC television documentary with historians David Starkey and Nicholas Clapton; these can support your efforts to teach about the economic and artistic circumstances that led thousands of boys to go under the knife in hopes of dazzling careers on the stage.[6] The rise of the castrati is invariably linked to Roman Catholic rules from the 16th century that prohibited women from singing in church, which made it challenging to include high voices in choirs. Few pre-pubescent boys could keep pace with adult singers, and in any case, their soprano lives were short, ending abruptly and unpredictably when their voices broke. Castration was an inventive way to preserve the male singer's high range past childhood, and this approach allowed church choirs to exploit the full, multi-octave range of the human voice, with altered males standing in for women.

These singers then also became active in the emerging genre of opera, and by the late 18th century, an elite number of castrati were the dominant stars of the operatic stage, particularly in dramatic, serious works. Descriptions of the castrato voice from its heyday remark on its intriguing strangeness, piercing, brilliant timbre, astonishing volume, wide range, and capacity for virtuoso feats of singing. The appetite for castrato voices diminished considerably through the 19th century, but Alessandro Moreschi (1858–1922) lived into the age of recording and his voice can be heard online in works such as Gounod's "Ave Maria."[7] In sharing this recording with students, though, you should brace for some disappointed reactions. It is worthwhile to remind your class that Moreschi, aged 46 at the time of recording, was past his prime singing years, and also that recording technology of the time tended to distort sound (particularly high sound). In short: Moreschi may have been the last of the castrati, but his recordings probably do not represent the best of the castrati.

If the castrato innovation was, at first, a purely pragmatic way to get high voices into church music without female bodies attached to them, then it is striking that when castrati took center stage in the opera world, they rarely performed female roles. Rather, castrati were deployed as allegorical figures (i.e., "La Musica," or "Esperanza") or as mythical heroes such as Achilles or Jason, roles in which their uncanny, otherworldly voices offered a sublime contrast to the ordinary mortal characters. Francesco Cavalli's 1649 *Giasone* was one of the most popular operas of the century, while the story of Achilles got the operatic treatment by dozens of composers including John Gay (in London) and Niccolò Jomelli (in Naples). In both cases, the heroic title roles were performed by castrati. Although it is not prominent on today's operatic stage, the story of legendary hero Achilles was particularly popular during the castrati vogue, perhaps because it already involved genderbending and masquerade. In classical Greek myth, the boy Achilles was disguised as a girl because his mother feared a prophecy that he would die in battle, and he betrayed his masculinity through picking up a sword rather than a necklace when offered a choice of wares for sale. For a male performer who sang like a woman, then, the role of Achilles presented intriguing possibilities for destabilizing binaried gender expectations.

The Achilles operas are difficult to teach, unfortunately, because they are seldom performed today. By contrast, Handel's 1724 opera *Giulio Cesare* premiered in London and remains in the standard repertory, meaning that there are many accessible resources for teaching.[8] The plot presents Julius Caesar's love story with Cleopatra against a backdrop of political tension and military conflict. In Handel's original cast, the major male roles of Caesar, the hero, and Tolomeo, the villain, were written for castrato singers, while a female soprano debuted the role of Cleopatra and another woman performed the part of Sesto, a young boy. This opera thus relied on several gender-bending performances in order to be brought to life, and it offers a fascinating case study for teaching about gender in 18th-century Europe as well as in contemporary settings.

In the absence of castrato singers today, producers of *Giulio Cesare* who want to hew close to 18th-century performance practice can adopt one of two strategies in casting the title role: a female mezzo soprano

Performance 73

or a male countertenor. Each option presents exciting provocations to rigid gender norms, all the more acutely because the historical figure of Julius Caesar is famous for his military skill, political dominance, and other attributes conventionally deemed masculine. What does it mean for audiences today to hear a high, light voice setting out military strategy and issuing orders to soldiers? How can contemporary listeners make sense of Baroque conventions of masculine authority that seem so different to the ideals of manhood we have been taught are natural and immutable? A discussion based on comparing performances can address these and other intriguing questions.

The German countertenor Andreas Scholl is admired for his interpretation of Caesar, and he has performed the role in productions at several of the world's leading operatic stages; likewise, the English mezzo soprano Sarah Connolly played the role in an award-winning production at the Glyndebourne Festival Opera. Good quality film versions exist online of both performers singing "Empio, Dirò, Tu Sei" with full sets and stage action, and these clips can be useful in class.[9] This aria appears in the first act, when the Egyptian army commander has presented Caesar with the head of his own general, Pompeo; the box has been opened in front of Pompeo's widow and son. The aria must be a bravura performance of scorching rage, condemning the cruel act with such force that Caesar makes everyone believe in his strength and dominance. Anger is an emotion invariably associated with masculinity—indeed, it is sometimes the only emotion permitted to boys and men, while girls and women are commonly socialized to avoid seeming angry—so this performance immediately confronts our implicit biases about gender presentation.

Travesti

Handel's cast for *Giulio Cesare* featured castrato singers in the principal male roles of hero and antagonist (there is additionally a minor role for a third castrato), and he also cast a female soprano in the role of Sesto, the young son of the unfortunate Roman general Pompeo. Sesto is thus a travesti or "trouser" role that requires a woman to dress in male attire and play the part of a man while singing in her comfortable female range. Since his is a minor role in an opera that revolves around castrati as lead characters, Sesto is not representative of the strategy of replacing castrati with women singers that began in the late 18th century. As appreciation for castrati voices waned, female sopranos and mezzos began to take on their heroic roles in serious operas, and Naomi André analyzes the ways in which this kind of cross-dressing heroism challenged conceptions of femininity as docile and fragile.[10] Because many star singers would perform delicate heroines in one opera and bold heroes in another, travesti singers performed a fluidity with gender that will intrigue students who may believe that gender roles were rigid and unshakable before the 21st century.

The most popular travesti roles in the repertory today, such as Mozart's Cherubino in *Le Nozze di Figaro* or Octavian in Strauss's *Der Rosenkavalier*, are not heroes or rebels, however. Rather, they are boys in the midst of adolescent hormonal surges and awakening libidos. The women who portray these immature boys present audiences with a spectacle of gender in transition, fraught with possibility and delightful confusion. In the 18th and 19th centuries, the mere sight of a woman wearing trousers was titillating, as Laurence Senelick explains in his history of transvestism in theatre.[11] The travesti characters of romantic and comic operas are figures of sexual desire and desirability, and gender fluidity is central to their appeal.

Cherubino is emblematic of this kind of role; he is a sex-crazed boy who swoons over all women in his reach, and he gets passively dressed up as girl, on stage, by two women, in just one of many risqué escapades. And while the character of Sesto may be costumed to look as much like a real boy as possible, singers chosen to play Cherubino are often tasked with appearing ultra-feminine while in male attire, highlighting the layers of artifice and winking at the audience. Within the plot of *Le Nozze di Figaro*, Cherubino is mischievous and charming, upsetting all the rules of social order and decorum, including gender.

Mozart's beloved comic opera (1786) was based on a famous 1778 play by Pierre Beaumarchais about the exploits of servants and their countess foiling the predatory sexual appetite of Count Almaviva, who hopes to sleep with his wife's maid, Susanna, prior to her marriage to his valet, Figaro. In Beaumarchais's play, the role of the pageboy Chérubin was portrayed by an actress in trousers—indeed, the playwright's stage directions insist that the role should be played by a pretty, young woman.[12] Clearly, the casting of a soprano in the operatic version is not just about getting the right kind of vocal range; rather, "this young woman dressing as a man dressing as a woman was explicitly about sex."[13]

Like Cherubino, the role of Octavian in Strauss's 1911 *Der Rosenkavalier* presents the audience with the spectacle of a woman pretending to be a boy who pretends to be a girl. Octavian's lust for women, however, is unambiguously consummated, and the character performs a passion more intense than Cherubino's puppy love. Writing in decadent, *fin de siècle* Germany, Strauss was able to depict Octavian in daring and sexually explicit ways, and the opera actually opens with the character waking up in bed with an older, married woman. A contemporaneous reflection noted that it would be impossibly scandalous to present this scene with a man in the role and mused also that a female Octavian ensures we can see the character's sexual appetite as sweet rather than wolfish.[14] The sexiness of the travesti character inspires Australian scholar Margaret Reynolds to write about taking a woman on an early date to see *Rosenkavalier* "because where else can you see two women making love in a public space?"[15] Thus, the travesti singer offers a limited kind of representation to gay women and invites all in the audience (and on the stage) to feel sympathy with, not disapproval of, the experience of desire.

Pantomime Dames and Principal Boys

Male roles for women singers are an important thread in the history of opera, then, but the world of British pantomime, long considered a wholesome, accessible family entertainment, goes further. The stock character of the Principal Boy is always played by an attractive young woman, and the Dame, played by a conventionally masculine, cisgender older man, is also standard in pantomime casts. In the context of pantomime's slapstick comedy, social commentary, and improvisatory banter with the audience, gender confusion is among many *doubles entendres*. The dame and the principal boy are presented in ways that underscore their cross dressing; principal boys wear costumes that reveal their legs and exaggerate their curves, while dames speak and sing with deep, rough voices or make a show of adjusting their false bosoms and hips. Whether in the role of Mother Goose, Widow Twankey, or one of Cinderella's ugly stepsisters, the dame is generally played for laughs as a "middle-aged woman with uncontrollable sexual desires" who is frequently the mother of the principal boy.[16] In the pantomime *Aladdin,* then, the title character is played by a girl in tights while her mother is played by gruff old man in drag.

While principal boys are pretty, a pantomime dame presents a grotesque caricature of an old woman that exaggerates the performer's masculine traits; garish lipstick contrasts with visible chin stubble, and attempts at coquettishness are hilarious in their repulsiveness. In failing to pass, pantomime dames invite audiences to laugh at cross dressing, thus, perhaps, softening the threat of gender fluidity. The carnivalesque, topsy-turvy pleasures of the pantomime are not widely familiar outside of Britain, but the genre presents a fascinating example of anti-élite entertainment for the whole family, that is paradoxically built on bawdy humor and sendups of class and gender conventions.[17] Even in places where pantomime is little known, students are likely to recognize many of the performance strategies, their origins in *commedia dell'arte* traditions, and their legacy for operetta and musical theatre. Operetta roles such as *Die Fledermaus's* Count Orlofsky are conventionally played by women, while the 20th-century musicals *Chicago* and *Hairspray* are among several that include roles for sex-starved older women played by male actors.

Characters like these are neither as dignified and heroic as castrato roles like Giulio Cesare nor as sexy and alluring as Cherubino or Octavian, but they do offer ways to satirize hegemonic gender roles and to deflate their power. Through playing a pantomime dame, a cisgender male actor can shrug off the rigid confines of masculinity and revel in outrageously effeminate behavior. Even when these performances are temporary escapes, they allow the actor to try on behaviors that are normally off limits, and to point out the artifice of gender.

Voices in Transition

More than instrumentalists, singers' relationships to their bodies are critically important, and the vocal apparatus is merely one of the tools a singer uses in their art. The frisson produced when the singer's sound doesn't match their appearance is at the heart of cross-dressed performance, and the cognitive dissonance can spark reflection on the meanings of gender for those who hear. For those who transition gender and sex entirely, singing takes on a special significance, with the voice serving as an audible marker of physical and spiritual transitions.

Canadian singer Lucas Silveira, the first out trans man to be signed to a major record label (Warner), documented the changes in his singing through transition, creating a sonic journal of his journey into masculinity on the YouTube channel for his band, the Cliks. Silveira was already an established singer/songwriter before coming out as transgender, so his voice was crucial to his professional persona and to his sense of self. During his transition, he was unnerved by the experience of not recognizing his own voice, and he found reassurance in singing songs that were familiar. Over the course of four years, he sang through the shift toward living as a man and then through further shifts with hormone therapy. The recordings he made through this period are a valuable archive and a pedagogical project through which Silveira educates fans about gender transitioning.[18] The hormone testosterone deepens his voice, but songs recorded prior to hormone therapy indicate Silveira was already developing a bright, tenor quality and singing in range that many female singers would find uncomfortable. As US scholar Elias Krell notes, Silveira recorded Roy Orbison's "Crying" pre- and post-transition (in 2009 and 2012), and the two versions reveal differences in range, but also timbre and resonance.[19] Careful listening can inform a rich discussion about the mutability of the male voice.

"Crying" required Silveira to engage with his falsetto register, which was compromised by the impact of testosterone. Almost all people, including women, can use their falsetto in speaking and singing, but the sound is most distinctive in male voices. Falsetto singing is central to genres such as R&B, barbershop, bluegrass, and yodeling as well as in classical music. Among white US singers, Roy Orbison was admired for his light, floating falsetto, as was Brian Wilson of the Beach Boys, while Frankie Valli of the Four Seasons cultivated a brighter, piercing falsetto sound. In Black male gospel singing, falsetto singing occupies an important position in the performance of a range of masculinities in Black Pentecostal and Baptist communities.[20] The ecstatic, soaring falsetto singing of Marvin Gaye, Philip Bailey, Prince, the Weeknd and many others is a legacy of this model of Black masculinity, even amongst singers not raised in the church.

Some men use the falsetto register exclusively even after puberty offers them access to lower pitches that are conventionally masculine and authoritative, and this kind of vocality has been pathologized as a voice disorder called puberphonia.[21] When puberphonia is diagnosed, it is generally considered a psychological condition brought on by unresolved trauma, such as childhood abuse, that causes the singer/speaker to resist adulthood.[22] But might we also consider that a commitment to falsetto registers can be a healthy presentation of gender that signals possibilities beyond the conventional?

Reflections and Connections: Voicing Non-Binary Identities

The voice is at the center of discussion in this sample lesson on gender non-conforming musicians, because the voice is located in the body and is thus intimately connected to everyday gender presentation. Indeed, the voice is often considered an emblem of reality and sincerity, something that is "true" even when appearances lie. Much of the prejudice against trans people involves the notion that they are somehow deceitful, and that transitioning gender may be a treachery worthy of punishment. In genres such as country and folk music, sincerity and unmediated expression of truth are core values, and these genres are commonly perceived to have conservative and essentializing notions of gender that breed hostility towards difference. Yet country music style is attractive to many trans artists, as Shana Goldin-Perschbacher shows. An artist such as Albertan Rae Spoon describes themself as a "transgender country singer," and songs such as 2011's "I'll Be a Ghost For You" draws on musical imagery of lonesome cowboys to express the solitude of trans existence.[23] Their music thus complicates easy assumptions about genre as well as gender.

Spoon chose not to pursue the hormone therapy that would have brought about shifts in voice and physicality and brought them closer to a masculine presentation. This refusal of the gender binary is mirrored, perhaps, in their musical rhetoric; they use the tools and strategies of techno and electronic dance music just as comfortably as acoustic guitar and other sounds of country. In a 2013 documentary-musical by Chelsea McMullan, *My Prairie Home*, Spoon muses on their coming of age in rural Alberta, identifying clearly as both country and non-binary.[24] The film includes musical performances that combine electronic sounds with Spoon's clear folksinger voice, and visual imagery that juxtaposes traditional activities such as hunting with magic and the uncanny.

Spoon and other singers insist on the voice's capacity to queer gender norms and expand the horizons of identity, reminding us powerfully and bravely of the wide spectrum of human bodies and sex categories. Rather than shifting from one side of an imaginary gender binary to the other, singers over several centuries and across several genres and styles have poked holes in the very notion of simple, stable sex categories. The examples considered here demonstrate that the possibilities for creating music are always contingent on social norms and historical context, as performances of gender are always in dialog with what is and is not permissible. These voices provoke our thinking about the fluidity and infinite variety of the gender spectrum.

Sample Lesson Nine

Swan Lake

Tchaikovsky's first ballet, *Swan Lake,* premiered in Russia in 1877, and it is now, arguably, the single most famous and beloved ballet in the repertoire. Its story involves yearning for connection, love, betrayal, death, and transfiguration, all told without a word of dialogue through Tchaikovsky's beautiful music and graceful choreography by Petipa and Ivanov. Although music scholars will categorize Tchaikovsky as a Romantic composer, dance historians consider *Swan Lake* a classical ballet, as it was created in an epoch that saw the establishment of conventions that continue to be relevant today. A ballet like *Swan Lake* is meant to dazzle with sweeping, dramatic music, gorgeous sets and costumes, and the amazing spectacle of rows of identical ballerinas in identical costumes making identical movements in order to tell a story. For teaching purposes, the Kirov Ballet's 2012 production is an excellent online resource that allows viewers to imagine themselves in the theatre, hearing and seeing this artwork unfold on a huge stage with an orchestra pit below.[25] I strongly recommend asking students to watch at least one act of the ballet in its entirety (Act II stands alone well), and perhaps organizing an online watch party, or an in-person viewing on a large screen if that is feasible.

Spectacle and Scopophilia

Perhaps more than any other performing art form, ballet is about spectacle and scopophilia, the pleasures of looking. As a form of dance, ballet has its origins in Renaissance Italy and was developed and professionalized in France in the 18th century. At this point, ballet became a performance dance style (as distinct from social dance) and then developed into an increasingly virtuosic and athletic form through the 19th and 20th centuries in France and Russia. In productions on the world's leading ballet stages to this day, *Swan Lake* upholds ballet's emphasis on grace, discipline, and uniformity, often featuring a large *corps de ballet* of ballerinas chosen for their symmetrical body shapes and ability to perform identical movements with precision.

Because ballet tells stories through gesture and without words, its language of choreography reflects and reinforces well-worn conventions of gender. Through its hundred years' history as an art form, ballet has always been in conversation with contemporaneous conventions of gender and bodies, so it is "a superb site for observing Western rules for gendered and sexed behavior."[26] There are particular ways for women to dance—light, floating arms, a semblance of weightlessness through standing *en pointe* with all the body's weight balanced on the tips of the toes—and for men to dance—athletic leaps, grounded strength, and the ability to lift ballerinas through the air.

The physical demands of ballet increased significantly through the 20th century, and it is highly instructive to compare photos of two of the most famous ballerinas who have danced the principal role in *Swan Lake*. Anna Sobeshchenskaya, who debuted the role of Odette in the 1877 première, is pictured standing gracefully, in a knee-length skirt, one foot fully on the ground, and soft, plump arms that curve demurely around her waist.[27] When English ballerina Margot Fonteyn performed the role in 1967, by contrast, the expectations for ballet meant that she needed a very thin and muscled body. In photos, we see that she balances all her body weight on the tips of her toes, and her tutu is high enough that we can see her whole leg turned out from the hip. The juxtaposition of images efficiently communicates how ballet put more and more demands on dancers, requiring greater feats of athleticism and virtuosity with an insistence on looking graceful and effortless. The cliché about the beautiful ballerina smiling while her feet bleed inside the slippers is an indication of how demanding this art form is. What is the impact, for viewers of all genders, of endlessly repeating the idea that beauty and grace involve suffering?

Swan Lake: Story, Music, and Movement

The story of *Swan Lake* is drawn from a few Russian and German fairy tales, and the tale is about a prince, Siegfried, who is anxious about taking on adult responsibilities such as marriage. While out hunting with friends, he meets a girl named Odette who is among a group of young women cursed to be swans by day, revisiting their human forms only by night. Odette and Siegfried fall in love, but she remains demure, telling him they must separate when she returns to swan form. Later, Siegfried awaits Odette at a ball, but the wizard Rothbart, who is responsible for the curse, disguises his own daughter Odile to look like Odette and sends her instead. Siegfried declares his love for the false Odette, who has entranced him with her sexual brazenness, thereby cursing the real Odette to be a swan always. When he realizes his mistake, Siegfried finds the virtuous Odette by the lake; in some productions, they choose suicide under the water together, or the ending can imply that Siegfried's remorse has broken Rothbart's spell, so that he and Odette achieve a happy ending.

The contours of the story pit two versions of the swan girl against one another, according to the familiar Madonna/whore dichotomy of good = docile and nonsexual, bad = predatory and sexually knowing. Tchaikovsky's orchestral score follows well-established conventions for ballet writing, and he supplies beautiful, infectious melodies with light textures and steady rhythms. The scale of the orchestration is symphonic, and there is a great deal of repetition, as specific characters' themes weave through the four acts of the story like leitmotifs.

The enduringly popular "Flight of the Swans" theme appears first at the end of the first act, when the prince and his friends see a flock of swans in the air. The music is graceful and sorrowful, with oboe heard over fluttering harp and tremolo strings in B minor; the melody seems to fall back and then rise tentatively, with several ascents and falls over the trembling strings, and then brass instruments enter to add more strength and vigor. For a few measures, the melody shifts from a steady duple rhythm into triplets, in an achingly lovely expression of yearning and frustration. This theme becomes the motto for Odette's tragic, long-suffering character, portraying her beautiful melancholy and her tentative, yet doomed, efforts toward happiness. It is strongly associated with gender stereotypes of the graceful ballerina whose ethereal presence emerges from heartbreak and pain.

The musical score is only one dimension of ballet's narrative, of course, and you can help your students recognize the strategies of musical storytelling by examining movement. Dance tells stories without words, and dance gestures work with music to communicate information about characters in the story; consider how the melody of the "Flight of the Swans" theme corresponds to the leaping and falling of the dancing swans. Although much of this ballet revolves around extended dance scenes showcasing the ballet dancers' agility and poise, there are also segments in which dancers present something like wordless dialogue, and these scenes are instructive. In the first act of the Kirov Ballet production, for example, we see the prince and his mother in silent conversation; how do their gestures help us understand their relationship? The mother character moves in ways that show she is older and dignified, and the prince's gestures show he is respectful of her. We see also that Siegfried moves quite differently with his friends than he does with his mother, or with the character of his tutor, so this range of movement styles gives us some insight into his psychological state. The Kirov Ballet production provides some closeups so that we see facial expressions, but by and large ballet has to show intimacy and inner emotions through full body movement, and through projecting a character's inner feelings onto an ensemble dancing what is in the character's mind.

The music Tchaikovsky wrote for the ballet is different from the language he used in writing symphonies or chamber music; the point of ballet music is that it has to play a supporting role, it has to inspire elegant movement, and it has to be emotionally affecting and memorable. Your students may be intrigued and moved by a viral social media clip from 2020, showing an old Spanish woman listening to the main *Swan Lake* theme and being transported back to her life as a ballerina. The woman, Marta Gonzalez, had danced the role of Odette in the 1960s, and she was in the last stages of living with Alzheimer's when this video was made. In it, we see that although her memory is gone and she is very frail and bound to a wheelchair, the powerful musical theme connects her right back to the choreography her body remembers.[28] The clip makes a compelling case for the power of music in stimulating memory, and also reveals the gestural language of feminine beauty.

Swan Lake and Girl Culture

Many of your students will recognize the "Flight of the Swans" theme, and other music from the ballet, because they first encountered *Swan Lake* as children. The fairytale story has been endlessly appealing to children, and ballet in general is central to girl culture; in a foundational text of girl studies scholarship, British cultural theorist Angela McRobbie wrote about the function of dance as an appropriate source of fantasy for girls.[29] Through dreams of ballet, girls conform to normative ideas of feminine grace and prettiness, but they can also find enormous pleasure and joy in expressing themselves through their bodies. Texts such as Noel Streatfeild's 1936 book *Ballet Shoes*, the 2001–2009 pre-schoolers' television program *Angelina Ballerina*, and above all, 2003's computer-animated fantasy film *Barbie: Swan Lake*, have become enduring touchstones of girl culture.

It's easy to see why the story of *Swan Lake* would fit well into a culture that teaches girls to strive for beauty, grace, and ethereality, because those are the qualities of a swan. Swans are admired for their snowy white feathers, their long, thin necks, and the way they can arch their wings elegantly up over their backs while they glide across the water—they seem almost tailormade for ballet. The *Swan Lake* story also places a lot of importance on the idea of true love, like many fairy tales which end with a wedding and living happily ever after, so *Barbie: Swan Lake* capitalizes on that too. Some of your students will have watched the film repeatedly as children, and it can be worthwhile to think about the impact this story had on their senses of self, particularly with regard to femininity. It's common to feel embarrassed about the things we liked as children, and society tends to be particularly dismissive of the things that girls like, but it is possible to find things to admire in *Barbie: Swan Lake*. True, the CGI animation is crude by contemporary standards, and the dialogue and characters lack the depth that adults watching alongside their children might long for, but the message about finding courage within is positive. Above all, the character of Odette, as "portrayed" by Barbie, has a back story and considerably more depth of character than Tchaikovsky's version, a tragic and beautiful doll in need of rescue.

Matthew Bourne's *Swan Lake*

Tchaikovsky and Petipa/Ivanov's Odette is a cipher; we never even learn who she was prior to Rothbart's spell or why she was bewitched in the first place. Her character is two-dimensional, in contrast to Siegfried, whose internal turmoil and tense relationship with his mother are given much scrutiny. Furthermore, the increased athleticism and stylization of ballet through the 20th century ensured that the figure of the ballerina solidified into an ornament, a beautiful but unattainable figure who is not quite human. In most productions, when Siegfried and Odette dance together he "does not so much desire Odette ... as he displays her. Through a series of lifts, supports, and manipulations, he *features* her to an audience ..."[30] There is little sexual chemistry between the two lovers, as they are stylized and prettified past the point of being humanly sexual.

But if the figure of the swan is easily connected to dominant ideas of feminine beauty and grace, and divorced from eroticism or desire, there is also another way to look at swans. They are huge birds, very strong, and can be quite aggressive; they are known to attack humans if they're defending a nest, and the idea of a swan strong enough to break a man's arm with their wings is an enduring urban myth. This version of swan-ness is also influential in the ballet world, because of the strength and agility required of male dancers. In particular, the British choreographer Matthew Bourne explored the masculine side of swans in an iconoclastic, multi-award-winning production of *Swan Lake* in 1996, in which all the swans were played by male dancers.

Bourne's production depicts another side of swans, fierce and intimidating, while retaining Tchaikovsky's music and many aspects of the original story. In this production, the swans are "bare-chested, barefoot, and hairy, with mounds of feathers around their thighs, [dancing] sharply and aggressively," and their movements remind us that swans are wild animals, in contrast to the tame creatures of conventional productions.[31] Typically, for example, the "Dance of the Cygnets," features four up-and-coming ballerinas elevated from the corps de ballet to demonstrate precise footwork and beautiful arabesques, to the accompaniment of quacking woodwinds. In Bourne's conception, four male swans evoke the movement of ungainly young swans more closely, with waddling and chest thrusting that matches the comical music more accurately. A comparison of versions of the "Dance of the Cygnets" will remind your students that the dancers are meant to be depicting birds, not dolls.[32]

This is subversive and exciting above all in its portrayal of the relationship between the Swan and the Prince; two male dancers of comparable strength and agility are able to ignite the taboo erotic connection between the characters. In their first dance together, for example, the Swan entices the Prince and then rebuffs him with a sudden high kick near his face, suggestive of the unpredictability and potential aggressiveness of wild swans, and the *pas de deux* unfolds with the dancers lifting one another. Through gestures that are recognizably drawn from everyday movement rather than the highly stylized and formal standard language of conventional ballet, Bourne and his dancers are able to communicate their story very effectively to audiences who may not have much familiarity with classical ballet.

Bourne's retelling of *Swan Lake* involves significant attention to the Prince's psychological state, his loneliness, and his unfulfilling relationship with a cold mother.[33] The attraction between the Prince and the Swan ensures that this version of the ballet can be read as a homoerotic relationship, or perhaps a story of recognizing queer sexuality. This kind of story, though it is told against the backdrop of Tchaikovsky's familiar music, has been seen as a provocative and radical statement about queer masculinity and dance.

Connections and Reflections: Billy Elliot

The notion that ballet is incompatible with "proper" masculinity is the premise of the film *Billy Elliot,* which was released as a film in 2000 and has subsequently been remade as a stage musical with songs by Elton John. The story is about a British boy who comes from a family in crisis—his father and brother are both miners, and the events take place against the backdrop of the 1984–1985 miners' strike that held out for more than a year before being crushed. Billy's mother has died and his father is trying to raise his sons while also dealing with the terrible stress of poverty and fighting for worker's rights. Billy develops an unexpected passion for ballet, and this leads, predictably, to conflict about manhood. There is also struggle about money and the extreme challenges for a poor working-class boy to enter the privileged world of a ballet school, but the film ends with Billy's father and brother sitting in the audience watching grownup Billy make his debut as a lead dancer. We hear Tchaikovsky's "Flight of the Swans" theme as Billy makes his first grand leap onto the stage, and we see his father's tear-filled eyes before the screen fades to black.

Swan Lake is probably the most famous ballet in the world—if people know only one ballet, it's likely to be this one—so we can interpret this final scene as meaning simply that Billy has made it into the highest ranks of the ballet world. Yet Billy is clearly costumed as a swan, not as Prince Siegfried, and all the other male dancers backstage with him are also dressed as swans. In fact, the dancer playing grownup Billy is Adam Cooper, who debuted the lead role in Bourne's production and also contributed to a lot of the choreography. For those viewers who know the ballet world, then, this final scene signals unmistakably that Billy is performing in Bourne's version of *Swan Lake* and that he has become professionally aligned with a new wave of ballet masculinities.

Your students may be pleased with the idea of making *Swan Lake,* and ballet more broadly, into something that can be more inclusive and flexible in assigning gender roles. In the last 50 years there has been a significant and important increase in support for girls who resist the rigid confines of femininity, and most people nowadays find it acceptable, even admirable, for little girls to be interested in things that are supposedly just for boys. But there has been less support and acceptance for boys wanting to do things that are stereotypically girly, such as dance. This is limiting at best and traumatizing at worst. I hope that you and your students can celebrate the concept of ballet playing a role in breaking down those damaging boundaries.

Using *Swan Lake,* the Billy Elliot story has launched the careers of Jamie Bell in the original movie and also Tom Holland, who played the role in the stage musical. Both of these actors are now adults who have talked about how the role of Billy helped them to understand themselves better and to feel comfortable and confident in nonconventional masculinity. So, like the Spanish ballerina mentioned earlier, it seems that dancing the role of Billy and the Swan has become hardwired into the physical memory of these men, and has helped them to change assumptions about masculinity more broadly.

Sample Lesson Ten

Disney Musicals and Compulsory Heterosexuality

Anyone who has spent time with young children knows their insatiable appetite for repetition. As adults, we tend not to remember our former enthusiasm for the same experiences and entertainments over and over, but we know that cries of "Again! Again!" are a constant refrain of childhood, responding to a favorite story, activity, or song. If a need for repetition is a constant aspect of childhood, then the possibility of automatic, exact repetition on demand is relatively new: only in the past few decades have children been able to hear their favorite recorded music or see their preferred television shows and movies as often as they would like. With the ease and availability of children's media on tapes, CDs, DVDs, and then streaming servers, a child growing up after the 1980s may absorb a cherished song or movie multiple times every day.

Among other media, children's animation draws on familiar images and characterizations in its storytelling, repeating stereotypes and idealized images that often reinforce gender and race identities. This coincides with the way that gender is learned and reproduced through repetition to the point that mimicry feels unconscious and natural. Through innumerable repeated viewings and hearings, children absorb lessons about gender and sexuality from cartoon characters and well-crafted, appealing songs. Overwhelmingly, children's media reifies conventional gender roles, with stories about adventure and friendship designed for boys and stories about romance aimed at girls. Male characters outnumber female characters significantly (especially in stories about animals or other non-human characters), female characters often have no goals beyond love or marriage, and "sexy" female characters appear just as often in G-rated children's films as in R-rated adult ones.[34]

A large-scale study by the Kaiser Foundation in 2010 found that children in the United States spent an average of 10 hours, 45 minutes each day with media, as compared with 7:45 a decade before.[35] In their study of media use among pre-schoolers, US sociologists Karin Martin and Emily Kazyak found that half of 600 surveyed parents reported their children watched Disney films repeatedly.[36] What messages are children absorbing from these films, about the world and the places they are expected to find in it? And what role does music play in these lessons?

Given the ubiquity of Disney and its colonization of childhood around the world, it is worthwhile to examine the messages and strategies of Disney animated musicals. In this sample lesson, I trace a history of the Disney princess persona as performed through animation and voice work, and I offer strategies for analyzing Disney's lessons about gender, sexuality, and romance. Through consideration of Disney's versions of the European fairytales of Snow White, Cinderella, Sleeping Beauty, and the Little Mermaid, we can see clearly how the ideology of romance and the importance of marriage are imparted to children from a young age. In films such as *Frozen*, by contrast, Disney stories offer fantasies that revolve around other important relationships.

Once Upon a Time: Snow White and the First Disney Princesses

Walt Disney's first animated feature film was 1937's *Snow White and the Seven Dwarfs,* based on a German folk tale collected and codified by the Brothers Grimm in 1812; it was deemed the greatest American animated film by the American Film Institute in 2008. At the time of its release, the film won an Oscar for its musical score, which was sold as a soundtrack album that could be played at home, while the film could only be seen in cinemas. *Snow White* was a landmark achievement for animation as a form, and the credits sequence names many artists who drew (by hand) the beautiful landscapes and compelling characters. Credit is also given to the composers, Paul Smith, Leigh Harline, and Frank Churchill, who created incidental music and wrote songs such as "Someday my Prince Will Come" and "Whistle While You Work."

Strikingly, the actors and singers who voiced the characters are not credited. This strategy helped to support the illusion of magic so important to Disney as a producer, as it erected a wall between the fairy tale characters and the mundane humans who spoke for them. Italian-American Adriana Caselotti, who voiced Snow White, imbued the character with a sweetness so distinctive that Walt Disney took steps to limit her other performing opportunities, in an effort to ensure Snow White was not heard outside of the world he had created for her.[37] Caselotti was a trained singer who came from a family of opera professionals—her sister was a teacher to Maria Callas—and her pretty soprano voice was a light and nimble match for Disney's vision of the character. With her graceful trills and portamentos, Caselotti gave Snow White a gentle, demure innocence that was attractive without being assertive.

The character of Snow White, of course, is meek and dutiful to a fault. Shunned and mistreated by her stepmother, this princess works as a drudge without complaint, singing and daydreaming contentedly with only birds for friends. Even after she has fled into the woods to escape murder by the queen, she ignores the warnings of her dwarf and animal friends, kindly welcoming a stranger who foists a poisoned apple on her. Through the film, she demonstrates that she is utterly incapable of standing up for herself and seeks only to please those around her while she waits for her prince to come. Her passivity is rewarded in the end—but she has to die first. Caselotti's voice is a critical aspect of this model of femininity, which teaches girls to practice patience and obedience above all.

Caselotti's silvery soprano voice was a good fit for this first Disney princess, and the songs written for her correspond to operetta and other genteel musical styles of the day. This kind of musical language ensured that *Snow White and the Seven Dwarfs* was embraced as a form of entertainment that was respectable and even edifying, yet not intimidating or overly ambitious. This vision of elevated, but still comfortably middle-class, culture would guide all Disney creations and would also shape its preferred depictions of femininity. Over the decades, though, different musical language and different voice types have helped Disney remain in conversation with social mores and the aspirations of their target audiences.

Cinderella and Sleeping Beauty

Despite the great success of *Snow White*, Disney would not create another princess-centered fairy tale film until 1950, with *Cinderella*. This film bears comparison with 1959's *Sleeping Beauty*; many of the same storywriters and directors worked on both, both take inspiration from French fairy tales involving long-suffering princesses and fairy godmothers, their heroines are visually similar blue-eyed blondes, and each depicts a love story leading to marriage as the happy conclusion. While the music for *Cinderella* was written by conservatory-trained composers and featured a pop singer voicing the main character, however, *Sleeping Beauty's* score was created by a composer who had learned his craft working in bands, and the princess's singing was done by an opera singer.

US actress Ilene Woods, the voice of Cinderella, began working as an actor at the age of two, and she hosted a radio program, *The Ilene Woods Show* at 15. Despite the lack of formal training, then, she was thus a seasoned professional at 19, when songwriters Mack David and Jerry Livingston hired her to record demos of their songs, including "A Dream is a Wish Your Heart Makes," for Walt Disney to consider for use in his upcoming Cinderella film. She was pleased when the song was chosen, and surprised to earn the role of Cinderella's speaking and singing voice solely on the basis of the demo, when so many singers had done formal auditions.

Woods's singing voice is warm and clear, and "A Dream is a Wish Your Heart Makes" sits comfortably in the octave around middle C, in contrast to the octave-and-a-half range of Snow White's "Someday my Prince Will Come." While Cinderella's song is accessible for little girls to sing along, the melody of Snow White's song is more challenging in terms of harmonic modulations and odd intervals, and the high A above the treble staff makes it difficult for a singer not trained in using the head voice. Corresponding to her less refined music, the Cinderella character is less docile than Snow White: although she endures mistreatment by her stepmother and stepsisters, she does grumble about the endless chores. In these ways, Cinderella is a more down-to earth, relatable character than the impossibly virtuous Snow White. It is appropriate that her singing is less virtuosic, for all that the songwriters based their melody loosely on Liszt's Transcendental Etude no. 9, "Ricordanza."

Aurora, the heroine of 1959's *Sleeping Beauty*, is a true princess like Snow White (and unlike Cinderella), and she is similarly voiced by an operatic singer, the Italian-American Mary Costa. Unlike the luckless Adriana Caselotti, however, Costa had a busy career before and after her work with Disney, singing coloratura roles such as Cunegonde (Bernstein's *Candide*) and Violetta (Verdi's *La Traviata*) on stages including the Metropolitan Opera and the Royal Opera House. In the summer of 1958, just prior to recording the role of Aurora, in fact, she made her debut at Glyndebourne in Ermanno Wolf-Ferrari's *Il Segreto di Susanna*, a little-remembered comic opera that celebrates the pleasures of smoking. Considering Disney's sabotage 20 years earlier of Caselotti's career opportunities for fear that other roles would somehow taint Snow White, it is puzzling that he would allow Costa to take this stage role. Does this indicate a relaxing of his control over performers toward the end of his life, or did he decide that the British opera world was so remote from his audience as to be irrelevant?

The music for *Sleeping Beauty* was based closely on Tchaikovsky's ballet of the same name, and the "Once Upon a Dream" duet and the "I Wonder" solo that precedes it both take their melodies from the Act I waltz for the princess's birthday celebrations. Aurora is in many ways the most operatic of the Disney princesses: she has very few lines of spoken dialogue, and her diction, breath control, and consistently beautiful tone through her whole singing range mark her character as refined even when she is living a simple life in the woods. In preparing for her duet with Prince Phillip, Costa rehearsed extensively with the tenor Bill Shirley (also a formally trained singer) to achieve a comfortable blend of voice. They also recorded hours of vocal sounds that were part of the reference materials for animators designing the characters, meaning that Costa contributed extensively to the sonic construction of this princess.

In the cases of all three of these first Disney princesses, the ability to sing well is a crucial indication of their goodness and beauty, in sharp contrast to the evil stepmothers or godmother who persecute them.

Their singing is also part of their ability to charm animals and speak with birds, bestowing a purity of character and a magical connection to nature.[38] The assignation of classical music style and actual melodic material connects these princesses to refined European culture, translated into the American vernacular that Disney would help to make a *lingua franca* for children's media around the world. The next generation of Disney princesses, however, would draw on new musical languages, borrowed from Broadway and pop singing.

Ariel and the Disney Renaissance

Even in their day in the early 20th century, the first Disney princesses were criticized for their passivity and reinforcement of the damsel-in-distress stereotype; feminists and others complained about the message that a girl could only find fulfillment in being chosen by a prince.[39] Through the socially turbulent years of second wave feminist activism of the 1960s, 1970s, and 1980s, the Disney empire held back from producing princess-themed films for children. In 1989, this changed with *The Little Mermaid*, based on an 1837 tale written by Danish author Hans Christian Andersen. This was the first Disney film with music by Alan Menken, whose score would win two Oscars and set the sonic template for what has been called "the Disney Renaissance." Menken went on to write music for Disney triumphs *Beauty and the Beast, Aladdin, Pocahontas, Tangled,* and *The Hunchback of Notre Dame*, all films which include a sympathetic heroine role (though she is not always a princess). In many important ways, though, the performance of princess-ness has changed significantly from Disney's earlier representations.

In terms of music, the new princesses expressed themselves in ways borrowed from Broadway musicals, not opera. Quite apart from the pronounced shift in singing style, the very structure and function of songs changed; where early princesses sang to other characters or animals who received their songs as performance, the new princesses would burst into song when their emotions grew so intense that mere words failed. As in the formula for Broadway, these "films are thus integrated musicals structured around pivotal moments designed to express emotional intensity and develop character."[40] And while Snow White, Cinderella, and Aurora entertained their friends with songs vaguely about romance and courtship, the new princesses use song to express their frustration about not fitting into their environments, and their longing to be somewhere—or someone—else, so that the bursting into song seems almost to bring about the change they long for.[41]

Structurally, these songs appear early in a musical story and serve to introduce the principal character and the conflict ahead, and US composer Stephen Schwartz opines that "I have learned over the years that pretty much any successful musical you can name has an 'I Want' song for its main character within the first fifteen or so minutes of the show."[42] The "I Want" song functions somewhat like the call to adventure in Joseph Campbell's phases of the hero's Quest, and in the context of a Disney princess musical, it automatically imbues the singer with agency and the possibility of heroism. This is already a striking departure from the passivity of earlier Disney princesses.

Ariel, the central character of *The Little Mermaid*, is a girl who is loved and protected at home, in marked contrast to the woeful Snow White, Aurora, and Cinderella. Nevertheless, Ariel introduces herself to the audience with a song about longing for adventure. White US actress Jodi Benson, who contributes Ariel's singing and speaking voices, was establishing a career as a stage actress on Broadway when she auditioned for the role, and she went on to voice the character in three films, a television series, and several video games. Benson's speaking work moves away from the refined, quasi-British diction of earlier Disney princesses, dropping "g"s at the ends of words and deploying folksy American grammar, and her singing is also speech-like. The melody of "Part of your World," for example, has a vocal range of just one octave spanning Benson's mid register, allowing the singer to shift easily from singing to speaking throughout.

Ideologies of Romance

Ariel's voice is central not just to her character, but to the plot of her story: the wicked witch steals it in order to trick Prince Eric into falling in love with the wrong girl, and Benson provides the voice for this false princess just as the same ballerina conventionally plays the roles of Odette and Odile in Tchaikovsky's *Swan Lake*. Ariel's voice, then, is her most important attribute, the emblem of her truest self, and the audience understands that Prince Eric is faithful to her even through his infatuation with Vanessa, because it is the voice that he loves. The irresistible allure of the princess's voice connects Ariel to Snow White and Aurora, as both of their princes were drawn to search for them on the basis of having overheard their singing. In this way, Disney princesses reify a notion of romance built on the idea of perfect soulmates and love at first sight—or sound. In these stories, a boy is instantly and infallibly drawn to the right girl when he recognizes her through her voice, and in the name of true love, he is automatically forgiven for invading her personal space through climbing over a wall (in *Snow White*), sneaking up on her through the woods (*Sleeping Beauty*), or breaking into her garden at night to whisk her away on a magic carpet (*Aladdin*). In response, the girl comes to recognize her prince and then gives in to his advances.

Let us not forget that this ideology of romance is directed at children, who absorb lessons about gender-appropriate attitudes and courtship behaviors as they watch, listen, and re-enact the songs and stories. In play-acting Ariel or other princesses, little girls adopt the vocal and physical attributes of women in the throes of falling in love, mimicking emotions and desires far in advance of feeling authentic, adult sexual desire. Thus, as award-winning US journalist Peggy Orenstein suggests, they will "learn that sexuality is something that you perform, instead of something that you feel."[43] These stories assert that romance and marriage are the most important (and in some cases, the only) goals for women, and that falling in love is so momentous that even birds and animals will invest energy into bringing about the perfect match! These stories are unrelentingly heteronormative, restricting the experience of love to young, cisgender, and able-bodied men and women, and thus regulating what children can recognize as possible.

Disney Princesses Grappling with Diversity

Alongside their princess films, of course, Disney has offered children many other kinds of animated musical stories. Films like *The Jungle Book*, *The Aristocats*, and *The Lion King* moved away from European fairy tales as source material and delighted audiences with appealing characters and songs that have nothing to do with romance. Notably, most of this style of film involves animal and other non-human characters, as do animated but non-musical films like the *Toy Story* and *Cars* franchises. Still, even these films often reinforce compulsory heterosexual romance and include sexualized depictions, as with O'Malley and Duchess in 1970's *The Aristocats* or Simba and Nala in 1994's *The Lion King*.

What is more, these animal characters involved different performers for their singing and speaking voices, following an established Hollywood (and Bollywood) convention in live action film musicals. In well-known film musicals such as *West Side Story* (1961) and *My Fair Lady* (1964), conservatory-trained vocalists provided the singing voices of characters otherwise performed by actors. Thus, the fact that Simba was performed by both actor Matthew Broderick and rock singer Joseph Williams, while Nala was voiced by Moira Kelly and singer/songwriter Sally Dworsky, is not dissimilar to *West Side Story*'s use of both movie star Natalie Wood and operatic soprano Marni Nixon for Maria, and actor Richard Beymer and singer Jim Bryant for Tony. The use of multiple voices allows greater depth and complexity of character, as well as facilitating the use of more challenging music. Some Disney characters are intended to be aspirational rather than relatable, after all.

The issue of relatability and the question of which children can and cannot see themselves in Disney film fare began to affect the company's creative choices in the 1990s. Animated musical films from this decade include 1995's *Pocahontas* and 1998's *Mulan*, both musical stories that revolve around a central young girl protagonist who is not white, and whose stories are not drawn from European folk tales. Like Ariel, Pocahontas and Mulan both sing "I Want" songs in their introductory scenes, but neither is a princess, and Mulan's story does not involve a romance at all. These films, as well as 1992's *Aladdin,* were groundbreaking in choosing protagonists of color, at least visually. The speaking cast of *Aladdin* was entire white, while *Pocahontas* and *Mulan* earned Disney some credibility by casting actors with ethnic connections to the stories they were telling: Irene Bedard is the Inupiat/Cree actress who played Pocahontas's speaking voice, and Mulan's speech was contributed by Chinese American Ming-Na Wen.

The singing for both these characters, however, was performed, respectively, by Judy Kuhn, a white US singer trained at the Oberlin Conservatory, and Lea Salonga, a Filipina actress and singer who had earned several awards for her Broadway performance in *Miss Saigon* before working with Disney. Salonga also provided the singing voice for Princess Jasmine in *Aladdin* before voicing Mulan, in a strategy that seems diametrically opposed to Walt Disney's protectionist notion of princess voices as highly individual and distinct. The move toward inclusivity was thus only partial and skin deep—or drawing deep. In the performances that audiences heard, Asian voices were treated as interchangeable, and the company balked altogether at using racially appropriate voices for the characters' most true and intimate singing voices.

2009's *The Princess and the Frog* was a more decisive commitment to representation, with African American Broadway star Anika Noni Rose playing the speaking and singing role of Tiana (though the role of the purportedly Middle Eastern prince, Naveen, was played by white Brazilian Bruno Campos). It is true that Tiana spends much of the film bewitched as a frog, thus limiting the opportunities for children to see a Black girl as the heroine of a fairy tale romance, but the musical language of New Orleans jazz ensures that even in frog form, Tiana and other characters are recognizably Black. Rose's performance, in speaking and singing, deploys an audibly Southern US accent, and her impressive belting technique reinforces the American-ness of Tiana even though the film based its story on a German fairy tale published by the Brothers Grimm. Naveen, the prince condemned to live as a frog until he is kissed by a princess, is a romantic hero on par with other Disney princes, and the film ends with a wedding at which Tiana is restored to her human self with a kiss.[44] The magical happy ending here is comparable to other Disney princess films, ensuring that Black girls are able to build fantasies around a pretty fairy tale princess who finds true love.

Reflections and Connections: Elsa and Anna

Still, the reliance on ideologies of compulsory romance remained at the heart of Disney films even as they attempted, cautiously and sometimes clumsily, to offer more inclusive fare. The idea of a Disney princess movie revolving, *de rigueur*, around romance and marriage was at last disrupted with 2013's *Frozen*. Elsa and Anna, voiced by Broadway star Idina Menzel and television actress Kristen Bell, respectively, are sisters who must overcome the dangers of magic to save their country and restore Elsa to her throne. The film does not merely sidestep the marriage plot, it actively repudiates it, as the story includes a handsome prince who turns out to be the villain of the piece. When Anna's heart is damaged and her life is at stake, then, the act of true love that saves her is her sister's kiss and willingness to die in her place. *Frozen* offers the drama and magic of a Disney fairytale without the reductive insistence on marriage as the inevitable solution to a girl's problems.

Bell and Menzel, who both trained at the Tisch School for Performing Arts at New York University, create compelling and nuanced characters through their singing and acting. Elsa's solo "Let it Go" is unmistakably the film's centerpiece, a bravura anthem that celebrates rejecting expectations and choosing freedom over conformity. Menzel's powerful belting voice is thrilling, and the song's melody builds in intensity to a triumphant climax. Rather than expressing longing and frustration, "Let it Go" articulates confidence as Elsa embraces her power. For children of all genders, "Let it Go" offers a satisfyingly dramatic way to express determination, resilience, and self-love.

Discussion and Assignments Questions

1 The figure of the swan has appealed to many artists in music and dance. French composer Camille Saint-Saëns included a musical depiction of a swan, for solo cello, in his 1886 *Carnaval des animaux* suite. Although this music was not created to support dance performance, Chinese-American cellist Yo-Yo Ma has collaborated with African American street dancer Lil' Buck in an extraordinary interpretation. How does Lil' Buck's dancing, dressed in jeans and sneakers, evoke the swan's strength and grace? How does this version of swan expand our thinking about masculinity, and about race in the overwhelmingly white world of ballet?[45]
2 Although Disney is indisputably the dominant force in children's media, they are not the only source of models for gender roles for children. Analyze a children's musical film or television program that is not created by Disney, and consider how its music depicts gender. What is the ratio of male to female and gender-neutral characters? In the case of non-human characters, how is gender signaled through visual and aural cues?
3 Children also embrace animated films that are not musicals, from Disney and otherwise. Even when characters do not burst into song, though, music plays an important role in communicating information about characters' gender, race, age, and class status. Consider the messages of wordless music in a children's film soundtrack, and how it depicts gender.

Notes

1. Judith Butler, "Performative Acts and Gender Constitution: An Essay in Phenomenology and Feminist Theory," *Theatre Journal* 40/4 (December 1988), 519–31: 519. Italics in original.
2. Philip Auslander, "Musical Personae," in *TDR* 50, no. 1 (2006), 100–119: 112.
3. José Muñoz, *Cruising Utopia: the Then and There of Queer Futurity* (New York: New York University Press, 2009), 1.
4. Roberta Barker, "'Not One Thing Exactly': Gender, Performance and Critical Debates over the Early Modern Boy-Actress," *Literature Compass* 6/2 (2009): 460–81.
5. Naomi André, *Voicing Gender: Castrati, Travesti, and the Second Woman in Early-Nineteenth-Century Italian Opera* (Bloomington: Indiana University Press, 2006).
6. BBC Four, "I Castrati," December 2014. https://www.youtube.com/watch?v=zqDEU0y9BSI, accessed January 19, 2022.

7. https://www.openculture.com/2016/06/hear-alessandro-moreschi-the-only-castrato-ever-recorded-sing-ave-maria-and-other-classics-1904.html, accessed January 20, 2022.
8. The Metropolitan Opera's 2013 production, for example, created an educator guide which can be useful in many classrooms: https://www.metopera.org/globalassets/discover/education/educator-guides/giulio-cesare/giuliocesare.12-13.guide.pdf, accessed January 19, 2022.
9. Andreas Scholl in Handel's *Giulio Cesare* (dir. Lars Ulrik Mortensen, Royal Danish Opera, 2005) https://www.youtube.com/watch?v=cI9nDGOfoOg, and Sarah Connolly in Handel's *Giulio Cesare* (dir. David McVicar, Glyndebourne Festival Opera, 2005), https://www.youtube.com/watch?v=Q9knbyIG3Jc. Both sites accessed January 20, 2022.
10. André, *Voicing Gender*, 89–102.
11. Laurence Senelick, *The Changing Room: Sex, Drag, and Theatre* (London: Routledge, 2000): 159–78.
12. Senelick, *The Changing Room*, 219.
13. Margaret Reynolds, "Ruggiero's Deceptions, Cherubino's Distractions," in Corrine Blackmer and Patricia Juliana Smith, eds., *En Travesti: Women, Gender, Subversion, Opera* (New York: Columbia University Press, 1995), 132–51: 140.
14. Roland Tenschert, quoted in Senelick, *The Changing Room*, 221.
15. Reynolds, "Ruggiero's Deceptions," 133.
16. Edwin Eigner, "Imps, Dames and Principal Boys: Gender Confusion in the Nineteenth-Century Pantomime," *Browning Institute Studies* 17 (1989), 65–74: 67.
17. There are numerous online archives with photos and other documents of pantomime history. The Victoria and Albert Museum offers this overview as a starting point: https://www.vam.ac.uk/articles/the-story-of-pantomime#:~:text=Pantomime%20has%20its%20roots%20in,cast%20of%20mischievous%20stock%20characters.&text=Harlequinades%20were%20mimed%20with%20music,pantomime%20for%20around%20100%20years., accessed January 20, 2022.
18. Craig Jennex and Maria Murphy, "Covering Trans Media: Temporal and Narrative Potential in Messy Musical Archives," in Stan Hawkins, ed., *The Routledge Research Companion to Popular Music and Gender* (New York: Routledge, 2017). 313–325.
19. Lucas Silveira, "Crying" (2009) https://www.youtube.com/watch?v=FnushdY4R_E and https://www.youtube.com/watch?v=kovDREyTIfQ (2012), both accessed January 22, 2022. Elias Krell, "Contours Through Covers: Voice and Affect in the Music of Lucas Silveira," *Journal of Popular Music Studies* 25/4: 476–503.
20. Alisha Lola Jones, *Flaming? The Peculiar Theopolitics of Fire and Desire in Black Male Gospel Performance* (New York: Oxford University Press, 2020).
21. Ingo Titze, *Principles of Vocal Production* (New York: Prentice Hall, 2000).
22. I have suggested that Michael Jackson's preference for speaking and singing in a high, breathy voice might be linked to puberphonia. This is not a provable theory, and I have offered it largely to refute widespread

speculation that Jackson was "chemically castrated" as a child to delay puberty. There is extensive, reliable evidence that Jackson could access conventionally male vocal registers when he chose. Jacqueline Warwick, "'You Can't Win, Child, But You Can't Get Out of the Game': Michael Jackson's Transition from Child Star to Superstar," *Popular Music and Society* 35/2 (2012), 241–59.
23. Shana Goldin-Perschbacher, "TransAmericana: Gender, Genre, and Journey," *New Literary History* 46/4 (Autumn, 2015), 775–803: 783.
24. The film is available for free streaming via the National Film board of Canada, at https://www.nfb.ca/film/my_prairie_home/, accessed February 2, 2022.
25. The Kirov Ballet, Tchaikovsky's *Swan Lake*, dir. Oleg Vinogradov (Leningrad, 2012). https://www.youtube.com/watch?v=9rJoB7y6Ncs, accessed January 24, 2022.
26. Suzanne Juhasz, "Queer Swans: Those Fabulous Avians in the *Swan Lakes* of Les Ballets Trockadero and Matthew Bourne," *Dance Chronicle* 31 (2008), 54–83: 55.
27. Photo found in Alastair Macaulay, "Swan Lake Discoveries Allow for a Deeper Dive Into Its History," *The New York Times*, Oct. 13, 2015. https://www.nytimes.com/2015/10/14/arts/dance/swan-lake-discoveries-allow-for-a-deeper-dive-into-its-history.html, accessed January 24, 2022.
28. https://www.youtube.com/watch?v=6-j5yeRDBaU, accessed January 26, 2022.
29. Angela McRobbie, "Dance and Social Fantasy," in Angela McRobbie and Mica Nava, eds., *Gender and Generation* (Basingstoke: Macmillan, 1984): 130–61.
30. Juhasz, "Queer Swans," 239.
31. Kent G. Drummond, "The Queering of *Swan Lake*," *Journal of Homosexuality* 45/2-4 (2003), 235–55: 236.
32. The Royal Ballet, "Dance of the Cygnets," *Swan Lake* (choreographed by Liam Scarlett, 2018), https://www.youtube.com/watch?v=0GsajWIF3ws, and https://www.youtube.com/watch?v=l8BqSKj1BTM, both accessed January 26, 2022.
33. A summary of Bourne's plot is found in Drummond, *Queering of Swan Lake*, 240–3.
34. Stacy Smith, Marc Choueiti, and Katherine Pieper, *Gender Bias Without Borders: An Investigation of Female Characters in Popular Films Across 11 Countries* (Geena Davis Institute on Gender in Media, 2010).
35. Victoria Rideout, Ulla Foehr, and Donald Roberts, *Generation M: Media in the Lives of 8- to 18-Year-Olds* (Kaiser Family Foundation, 2010), 2.
36. Karin Martin and Emily Kazyak, "Hetero-Romantic Love and Heterosexiness in Children's G-Rated Films," *Gender and Society* 23 (2009): 315–36.
37. Disney also paid Caselotti less than $1000 for her work, and he did not invite her to the film's premiere. Tim Lawson and Alisa Persons, *The Magic Behind the Voices: A Who's Who of Cartoon Voice Actors* (University of Mississippi Press, 2004), 106–7.
38. Jennifer Fleeger, "The Disney Princess: Animation and Real Girls," in *Mismatched Women: The Siren's Song Through the Machine* (New York: Oxford University Press, 2014), 106–36.

39. Lawson and Persons, *The Magic Behind the Voices*, 107.
40. Fleeger, "Disney Princess," 120.
41. Ryan Bunch, "Soaring into Song: Youth and Yearning in Animated Musicals of the Disney Renaissance," *American Music* 39/2 (Summer, 2021), 182–95: 183–4.
42. Stephen Schwartz, quoted in "Writing 'I Want' Songs for Musicals," https://web.archive.org/web/20140602201129/http://www.musicalwriters.com/write/stephen-schwartz/songs/i-want-songs.htm, accessed January 30, 2022.
43. Peggy Orenstein, *Cinderella Ate My Daughter: Dispatches from the Front Lines of the New Girlie-Girl Culture* (New York: HarperCollins 2011).
44. A thoughtful consideration of Disney princes is found in Ryan Bunch, *Soaring into Song*.
45. Among numerous performances that have been filmed around the world, see: https://www.youtube.com/watch?v=qfEYjKWJ56E, accessed January 27, 2022.

Further Reading

André, Naomi. *Voicing Gender: Castrati, Travesti, and the Second Woman in Early-Nineteenth-Century Italian Opera*. Bloomington: Indiana University Press, 2006.

Auslander, Philip. *In Concert: Performing Musical Persona*. Ann Arbor: University of Michigan Press, 2021.

Karlinsky, Simon. "Man or Myth?: The Retrieval of the True Chaikovsky." In *Freedom from Violence and Lies: Essays on Russian Poetry and Music*, edited by Robert P. Hughes, Thomas A. Koster, and Richard Taruskin, 339–45. Boston: Academic Studies Press, 2013.

Martin, Karin and Emily Kazyak, "Hetero-Romantic Love and Heterosexiness in Children's G-Rated Films," *Gender and Society* 23 (2009): 315–36.

McClary, Susan. "Soprano Masculinities," In *Masculinity in Opera*, edited by Philip Purvis, 33–50. New York: Routledge, 2013.

McClary, Susan. *Feminine Endings: Music, Gender, and Sexuality*. Minneapolis: University of Minnesota Press, 1991.

Thomas, Gary. "Was George Frederic Handel Gay?: On Closet Questions and Cultural Politics." In *Queering the Pitch: The New Gay and Lesbian Musicology*, 2nd Edition, edited by Philip Brett, Elizabeth Wood, and Gary C. Thomas, 155–204. New York: Routledge, 2006.

Walser, Robert. *Running with the Devil: Power, Gender, and Madness in Heavy Metal Music*. Middletown: Wesleyan University Press, 1993.

Wolf, Stacy. "Never Gonna Be a Man/Catch Me If You Can/I Won't Grow Up': A Lesbian Account of Mary Martin as Peter Pan," *Theatre Journal* 49/4 (Winter, (December, 1997): 493–509.

4 Reception

In music history, audiences are often neglected or, when they are acknowledged, treated with contempt for their inability to appreciate the most challenging work. Even without the inflammatory title assigned to it by an editor, Princeton University composer Milton Babbitt's notorious 1958 article argues that an audience is irrelevant to the composer as specialist.[1] Yet just a few years later and 50 miles away, Columbia University's theater critic and playwright Eric Bentley would write his famous definition of theatre: "A impersonates B while C looks on," codifying the audience as integral to the phenomenon.[2] No less elitist than Babbitt, Bentley was contemptuous of theater that appealed to the masses, yet he recognized the audience as a crucial aspect of performance; more important, even, than the playwright!

The philosophical distance between Bentley and Babbitt is enormous and fascinating, and it illuminates the interesting difference in pedagogical approaches to music and theater through the late 20th century. For our purposes here, suffice it to say that the important work of listening has been seriously overlooked in music studies, until thinkers like New Zealander Christopher Small reminded us that music is an activity that connects people through sharing the experience of musicking, in which audience is vital.[3] The phenomenon of music reception is more likely to be acknowledged in discussion of popular music styles, where, as the essays in Lisa Lewis's ground-breaking 1992 collection *The Adoring Audience* indicate, audiences are often heavily gendered, to the point that the "wrong" kind of audience can cause discomfort and embarrassment for musicians.[4] Thus, we know that the Beatles grew so frustrated with their legion teen girl fans that they withdrew from performing live; reinventing themselves as an arty studio band, they earned greater respect from adult male listeners. In a different example, many middle-class white males are drawn to the

DOI: 10.4324/9781003042655-5

power and swagger of hip hop artists articulating the trials of Black urban poverty, often to the bemusement of the rappers themselves. Music fandoms often divide us, yet also the power of music to unite listeners is undeniable.

Music is a tremendous force in our lives, with power over our emotions. Through listening to music, we can learn empathy for people who are not like ourselves, and—perhaps more commonly—we can learn about ourselves through witnessing how a musician performs something we have felt. Music offers endless possible roles for us to try on as we go about the unending work of forging our personae and finding our places in community. The cues that music provides about identity—race, gender, age, class, and more—are effective because we absorb them without effort and often without noticing. Thus, a sultry chromatic saxophone phrase in a film soundtrack signals that a female character is sexually adventurous, and a slow, melancholy horn evokes an image of a noble hero wearily facing overwhelming obstacles.

These musical tropes help us recognize particular kinds of characters, and as they gain currency through repetition, they begin to solidify into clichés that actually shape our notions of identity. As US philosopher Judith Butler has taught us, gender is a performance, an "identity instituted through a repetition of acts," and repeated *hearing* of gendered stereotypes plays no small part in reinforcing their apparent naturalness.[5] The repetitive use of clichés and stereotypes can make sexism, racism, homophobia, transphobia, and other forms of prejudice seem normal, as idealized images disconnect us from real ones. African American scholar Hazel Carby observes that the function of stereotypes is "not to reflect or represent a reality, but to function as a disguise, or mystification, of objective social relations."[6] The ways that we hear, and process what we hear, matter a great deal to how we understand the people in the world around us, and the work of audiences is crucial to the existence of music.

Clichéd images of music fans are highly classed; picture the hackneyed opera aficionado sneering and wincing upon hearing electronic dance music, and recognize that this stereotype serves to erect borders between music styles and to divide people. Conventional understandings of fans are also gendered, in ways that often reinforce toxic, binary notions of men as aggressive and competitive, and women as shallow and vapid. Often, the female fan is imagined as immature: furthermore, she is frequently regarded with contempt and assumptions that her passion for music is superficial and uneducated. Specific genres and styles of music appeal strongly to cisgender men, and these listeners often take pains to disassociate themselves from what they dismiss as the immature and unworthy fandom of young women.

Fandom in sports and in gaming culture, both indisputably male dominated arenas, commonly involves competitiveness and a focus on strategy for winning. These parameters can also be applied, to some degree, to the music and musicians principally associated with hegemonic masculinities. Many male fans of these styles will enjoy testing "fake fans" about their knowledge of musicians deemed worthy, and this gatekeeping can be particularly hostile when directed at women. Indeed, in a university class on rock music, the female instructor herself should brace for challenges to her authority and expertise, while her cisgender, heteronormative male counterpart will more easily be accepted as proficient.

The ways that we listen, and the ways that we imagine listeners and listener communities, have significant power. There are several styles and genres of music so intensely important to a listener's sense of self that slighting a favorite artist or work of music can be received as a personal attack. A module examining the role of audiences is crucial in a class that strives toward complete understanding of music as a social text.

Suggested Topics

In the lesson topics that follow in this section, I offer three models for exploring the complex ways that listeners engage with music. My examples address the remarkable ways that teenage girls have used music to build a girl culture and to articulate their desires and concerns, the complexities of heteronormative masculinity as it relates to fans of music and sports, and those male artists in light classical and pop styles who dedicate their art to middle-aged women—an overlooked and fascinating fan base.

Sample Lesson Eleven

Lisztomania and Its Echoes

What would a gender-conscious history of the invention of music stars and fandom look and sound like? This history could begin with "Lisztomania," an epidemic that afflicted European women who swooned and shrieked at the concerts of the Hungarian pianist Franz Liszt in the 1840s. It could also include Frank Sinatra's bobbysoxer fans, who caused great consternation about the force of unbridled teen girl sexuality 100 years later, and then move on to the more familiar tales of Elvis Presley and Beatles fans causing uproar with their unrestrained responses to their idols. In all of these cases (not to mention more recent boy band fandom), it is possible to see the wild behavior of fans as insurgence, in which the musicians' role is to provide an excuse for breaking free.[7] However, although it has been attractive to meditate on Liszt by comparing him to rock rebels and countercultural values, the lineage I will draw connects him instead to music communities considered sentimental and tame.

To begin with Franz Liszt (1811–1886) is to accomplish a few things that I consider valuable: it shows students an important aspect of music history that may be unfamiliar to many of them; it reveals patterns of listener behavior originating in the very early years of the Victorian era; and it places a canonical virtuoso/composer side by side with more recent stars of popular music styles. This can serve to demystify the aura of a Great Composer (and thus, by implication, the very idea of the Great Composer) and also to afford insights into the experience of fandom across several styles of music.

Lisztomania

Given the ways that historians of classical music have tended to elevate composition as the highest order of participation in music (and composition of non-texted music as the highest order of composition), it is scarcely surprising that many music history textbooks are clumsy in reconciling Liszt the composer with Liszt the showman. By contrast, audiences from his day to ours have been intrigued by Liszt's extraordinary fame as a performer and as a scandalous celebrity. His life story has been explored in major films, including Ken Russell's notorious 1975 *Lisztomania* (with The Who's Roger Daltrey in the lead role), and novels, such as Susanne Dunlap's 2007 historical romance for teens, *Liszt's Kiss*.[8] These fictionalized treatments focus on Liszt's romantic exploits and his sensational concertizing career, presenting him as a forerunner to 20th-century rock stars who wrote and performed music that sent audiences wild.

The historical record shows that Liszt was highly skilled at what we now call public relations, and that he was well aware of how his image—thin, pale, dressed largely in black, and with shoulder-length hair that he would toss away from his face while he played—affected his audience. In an 1842 cartoon by German illustrator Theodor Hosemann ("Im Concertsaale"), the handsome 31-year-old pianist is posed dramatically at the piano, while an overwhelmingly female audience crowds below the stage, swooning and throwing flowers. The contemporary press wrote in astonishment of women preserving locks of his hair, fashioning jewelry from piano strings that broke through his bombastic playing, and even cherishing his cigar stubs and the dregs from his tea. In reaction to witnessing this alarming female behavior at the time, the German poet Heinrich Heine coined the term "Lisztomania," likening the frenzy of feeling to a disease. US musicologist Dana Gooley reminds us more recently that, in the 19th century, the metaphor of "mania" linked the phenomenon of admiring Liszt to a contagious and dangerous medical condition, an association that had been much diminished by the time the term was revived in connection to the Beatles in the early 1960s.[9]

Heine also suggested that the fans' ecstasy was cynically cultivated by Liszt and his staff, who themselves were said to provide the flowers and laurel wreaths that women could toss to their idol during performances.[10] Whether or not Liszt worked as deliberately to manipulate his devotees as Heine charged, there is no question that he thought carefully about audience experience and the staging of his performances. Learning from his father's successes in managing his career as a child prodigy, Liszt is often credited with inventing the idea of the concert pianist, and with designing the solo piano recital. Beyond determining the kind of repertoire appropriate for recital performance, and playing impressively from memory, his innovations include the significant shift in the placement of the piano across the concert stage, rather than facing it. This ensured that "Liszt was completely visible, the audience could focus on his profile, his facial expressions, his gestures and his body language ... as he himself put it, "le concert c'est moi."[11] Liszt's attention to stagecraft, his skillful management of audience response, and his willingness to trade on his good looks were undoubtedly part of a paradigm shift in approaches to music-making, one that paved the way for superstars to follow.

The musical works of Liszt, and peers such as Paganini and Berlioz, may strike today's students as remote, and sophisticated to the point of being accessible only to elite audiences. It is therefore instructive to teach them that concerts by these artists were sensational, electrifying, and designed to appeal to a massive public, as concerts for ticket-buyers became increasingly important to a musician's capacity to have a career. Even Liszt's famous 1837 "piano duel" with rival virtuoso Sigismond Thalberg was a money-making opportunity for both pianists: the event was hosted at the Paris salon of Princess Cristina Belgiojoso, who sold tickets at 40 francs each.[12] In later years, Liszt's deepening religious faith (to the point of taking minor orders) reinforced his reputation for exquisite sensitivity and furthered the notion of art as a new kind of spirituality. Other musicians may have mocked his piousness, including his son-in-law Richard Wagner (who nevertheless accepted his financial aid), but he retained a devoted following.

Crooners

Liszt's transcendent technique at the piano was supported by developments in piano manufacturing, such as the double escapement action introduced by Erard, which enabled rapid repetition of the same note; this is comparable to the ways that crooners revolutionized singing in the United States during the 1930s with the invention of microphone technique. Through the work of singers such as tenor Rudy Vallée (1901–1986), crooning rose to prominence in the early 1930s, feeding an appetite for soft-voiced white men who performed tenderness with quavering, breathy sounds and a willingness to appear fragile, as American Studies scholar Allison McCracken demonstrates in *Real Men Don't Sing*.[13] Microphones enabled light, warbling tenors to sound as though they were singing directly into the ears of their listeners, creating a sense of intimacy with appealing, easily remembered melodies and bland, sentimental lyrics. This new kind of male voice was in stark contrast to singers projecting from the theatrical or operatic stage, offering mildness and ardent (but non-threatening) emotion instead of sonic muscularity and bravura, and its existence suggested the possibility of men who were uninterested in power.

While upholders of hegemonic, heteronormative white masculinity were aghast, many women were keenly interested. These singers could be heard via the radio, which offered "unprecedented public penetration into private space. Worse yet, crooners privileged their female listeners, addressing them as beloved individuals and offering them nothing less than an alternative masculine idol and ideal, one who served their desires and was available to them at the flick of a switch."[14] Crooners were adored largely *because* they rejected the hegemonic masculine norms of stoicism, emotional control, and independence by willingly performing their reliance on and care for women. Through their effusive love for and gratitude to mothers and lovers, crooners seemed to revel in an emotional vulnerability that listeners could enjoy in the comfort of their own homes.

The disembodied voice of the crooner cooing sweet nothings via the radio or phonograph thus enabled private fantasies, appealing to women too timid to throw flowers at a public concert, as Lisztomaniacs had done. These listeners, often derided and dismissed as old maids, lonely housewives, or menopausal empty-nesters, could imagine themselves as cherished and desired, without fear of rejection or ridicule from their dream lovers. They could also envision the qualities of an ideal manhood against which real men could be measured. Crooners like Vallée were also adored by queer male listeners, who could position themselves as the intended subjects of love songs that relied heavily on "I-you" pronouns, and who could also craft public personae based on this (barely) acceptable level of effeteness. Crooners thus provided a language that went some way toward empowering women and gay men to express their desires and hopes for alternative masculinities.

If crooning enabled the popularity of blithe, sprightly tenors in the early 1930s, it is surely significant that deeper voices like those of US singers Bing Crosby (1903–1977), and later, Frank Sinatra (1915–1998), would co-opt the style by decade's end. Crooning in the 1940s was characterized by smooth baritone voices that hewed closer to heteronormative conventions of manliness, combined with the emotional openness of their predecessors. Crosby crafted a reassuringly avuncular persona that mitigated significantly against the perception of crooners as sissies, while he sang flawless legato lines in a warm baritone. For his part, Sinatra developed a vocal technique built on the capacities of the new ribbon microphones, which afforded a greater range of nuance in dynamics and phrasing. These expressive tools offered a disarming intimacy and gentleness that was all the more thrilling because Sinatra's deep voice hinted at the presence of restrained strength and power.[15]

Significantly, Sinatra's fan base was younger than that of Crosby or of Vallée; in the early days of his career, he was associated with "the bobbysoxer," a new breed of teenage girl who wore short socks instead of proper stockings, and whose enthusiasms and infatuations amused and alarmed her elders. With unabashed shrieking and swooning over idols like Sinatra, bobbysoxers revealed an intensity of sexual desire that disturbed society's preferred understanding of girls as innocent and docile. Bobbysoxers, like their heirs the Beatlemaniacs, or NSYNC and KPop fans of later decades, signaled the clout and importance of young girls as an audience, and even denunciations of their antics depicted them as sexually nascent and attractive. To some, even the most annoying teenaged bobbysoxer brimmed with the promise of womanly desirability; a pert girl who, with the proper guidance, would someday be able to fulfill her duties as a wife.

Liberace, Manilow, and the Older Woman Fan

The middle-aged woman fan who had sighed and sobbed over Vallée in the 1930s had less value in the marriage market (to say nothing of the effete, sissy man), and her musical passions were more likely to be derided. Through the 20th century, this kind of fan has been associated with artists like white US entertainers Liberace (1919–1987) and Barry Manilow (b. 1943), who have been scorned by critics and tastemakers alike, even as their legion fans find their music moving and life-affirming. US musicologist Mitchell Morris writes of Manilow that "Every pitch, every gesture, every corny gag directed at the fans has usually seemed to show Manilow asking his fans, 'Do you like this?' and maybe even, 'Do you like me?'"[16] The naked eagerness to please flies in the face of rock culture's ethos of cool, and it undoes the ideal of artistic passion refusing to compromise or cater to pedestrian tastes.

Although he was born the same year as Mick Jagger and Jim Morrison and grew up in Brooklyn, Manilow took no interest in rock'n'roll music as it emerged in urban youth cultures around him. Instead, he found his way into the music industry by writing commercial jingles, and detractors often criticize his song catalog on the grounds that his music is too commercial, too easy, and direct to be sincere. Jingles must be instantly recognizable and catchy so that they can cement themselves into the memories of listeners. Above all, jingles must get to the point quickly and deliver a sense of satisfaction or comfort, so the musical language must be simple, direct, and singable; Manilow's jingle "I am stuck on Band-Aid, 'cause Band-Aid's stuck on me" is exemplary.[17]

In 1974's "Mandy" (not a Manilow original: it was written and recorded by Scott English as "Brandy" in 1972), a repetitive, stepwise melody fits comfortably within an octave and tumbles softly over piano and gently swelling strings, as Manilow performs remorse over having sent away a woman who "gave without taking." The effect is sweetly melancholy, as the pleasant musical language offsets the anguish expressed in the lyrics, and the song comforts the woman listener who feels similarly disregarded in spite of her selflessness. The women who made up Manilow's principal fanbase in the 1970s were of the generation analyzed in Betty Friedan's *The Feminine Mystique* in 1963, and they had been encouraged to devote themselves wholeheartedly into making their children and husbands happy. A decade on, their children were grown and their husbands had lost interest in romance, but they had no senses of self except as wives and mothers.

Songs like "Mandy" were a welcome message that their sacrifices had, in fact, been appreciated.

To youthful listeners fancying themselves as edgy and progressive, the soft pap of "Mandy" was the antithesis of cool. Manilow thus built an extraordinarily successful career out of pleasing fans who were overlooked in music cultures centered around innovation, rebelliousness, and coming of age. In so doing, he followed in the footsteps of Vallée and Liberace, whose smiling approach to piano virtuosity was a balm to his fans. Classical music purists decried Liberace's vulgarization of the idea of the piano virtuoso, often without acknowledging the ways that Liszt, the architect of that idea, had himself catered to his audience's desires. Fans of popular music also scorned Liberace's style as sentimental and vapid, and both groups were uneasy with his flamboyant, camp style and what it implied about his sexuality.

To his followers, Liberace's attraction derived from his ability to combine dazzling virtuosity at the piano with a mild-mannered ordinariness, seen in the unabashed delight and wonder he took in his wealth. Mothers of adult children formed a not-insignificant portion of his fan base, and these listeners tended to be profoundly moved by his mawkish devotion to his own mother, who often joined him on stage (or television studio set) to be serenaded and showered with attention. Liberace had considerable expertise with high art music, but he did not impose snobbish expectations on others, as US musicologist Ivan Raykoff notes: "'If I play Tchaikovsky, I play his melodies and skip his spiritual struggles,' he explained. 'I have to know just how many notes my audience will stand for. If there's any time left over, I fill in a lot of runs up and down the scale.'"[18] Liberace's cheerful willingness to carve up classical piano repertoire if it bored his audience was appalling to discerning listeners, who saw it as pandering to the lowest common denominator. To his fans, however, it felt like solicitousness and care.

Reflections and Connections: Kenny G and Smooth Jazz

Artists like Liberace, Manilow, and Vallée fit uncomfortably within conventional histories of music, because they willingly accept compromise in order to appeal to the wrong sorts of fan: women and soft men of a "certain age" with unsophisticated tastes. In creating music that soothes and reassures, they seem to abandon Romantic ideals of art for art's sake, and in privileging the tastes of listeners who are uninterested in hierarchies of judgment, they betray those who seek to police appreciation of music.

Yet the fans moved by Liberace's devotion to his mother or charmed by Manilow's tender ballads represent a large swath of society, often including our students' mothers, aunties, and grandmothers. What does it mean to despise their musical preferences? In his analysis of smooth jazz giant Kenny G, Robert Walser writes that "millions of people make love to Kenny G's music; it reassures, comforts, promotes tenderness. Empathetically read, Kenny G's music is also a critique; its particular kind of beauty is meaningful for many people because it protests a world of too little tenderness, not enough nuance, too few caresses."[19] In teaching a lesson about this kind of fandom and the musicians who serve it, you have the opportunity to awaken reflection in your students about gatekeeping and hierarchies of taste. Through investing time into music that they may initially recoil from, students can reflect on the ways that music offers comfort for unmet needs, and can recognize that even music they dislike may be cherished by people they love.

Sample Lesson Twelve

Girlhood and Pop Music

A focus on girls' music and musical constructions of girlhood can add an excellent dimension to a course that deals with music, gender, and sexuality. The interdisciplinary field of girl studies is vibrant and exciting, and—given the broad social contempt that continues to be directed at teenage girls—students will feel gratified and intrigued to see that the experience of girlhood is worthy of respectful engagement. Beyond the rewards of discussing girl culture, though, this lesson can inspire thinking about how music functions in the context of other subject positions, such as motherhood and fatherhood, childhood, old age, and more.

It is useful to distinguish the idea of girlhood from both womanhood and youth, and to stress that all of these are socially constructed positions. We must acknowledge that the term "girl" is often used pejoratively, to trivialize or demean people considered unworthy of being recognized as "women" or "ladies": this use of the term has a long history in racist and classist social hierarchies. Yet "girl" can also be a word that confers respect, affection, and sisterhood. In both these contexts, the term can be applied to or claimed by people of many genders and ages, but it also applies to a specific age and gender identity. These three interlocking meanings of the word "girl" are all relevant to a study of girlhood and music.

Building on the consideration of how clichés and stereotypes function, ask your students to identify some common stereotypes of teenage girls, and to analyze the power and meaning of these images. Why is the "mean girl" such an easy way to characterize girlhood? Are there classist and racist implications to the ways we habitually envisage "the girl next door"? This discussion can extend to a focus on stereotypes of girls' voices, addressing much-maligned vocal mannerisms such as uptalk and vocal fry. What is at stake in policing the ways that girls speak?[20] This class activity can lead to a lively and productive discussion about stereotypes and their power to limit people's opportunities; with the starting point of relatively benign clichés of white teenage girls as vapid, frivolous, and superficial, you may be able to help your students consider the dangers of other, more damaging stereotypes.

Girl Groups of the 1960s

A thorough history of girlhood and music could certainly include such canonical texts as Purcell's *Dido and Aeneas,* written for performance by students at a girls' school in Chelsea in 1689, as well as Vivaldi's works between 1703 and 1733, when he was employed creating music for the orchestra and choir at Venice's Ospedale della Pietà. However, a more streamlined approach to this topic, focusing particularly on reception rather than performance, can limit itself to music associated with and marketed to girls in the 20th century, beginning in the rock'n'roll era. This strategy allows you to start with the girl groups of the 1960s, a genre whose primary fanbase was teenage girls of the Baby Boom generation. Girl group singers and their fans were coming of age at a time when the notion of distinct youth culture was coalescing, and the music played a significant role in establishing codes and norms of adolescent experience which have resonated down the generations. The legacy of girl groups as emblems of girlhood enduring long after their heyday can be witnessed in such disparate texts as the opening credit sequence of the 1987 film *Adventures in Babysitting*; the Greek chorus in the 1997 Disney film *Hercules*; or Amy Winehouse's 2006 album *Back to Black.*

The girl group sound revolved around the audibly adolescent and pre-adolescent voices of girls, with professional songwriters and studio musicians supporting their untutored singing; girl group records were often more racially integrated than other contemporaneous styles of music. There are many well-loved examples that can represent the genre, but my recommendation, for the purposes of this lecture topic, is to choose songs that provided templates for "nice" girls learning to articulate their wants and needs in the early 1960s: the Shirelles' monumental "Will You Love Me Tomorrow?" (1961), the Crystals' "Da Doo Ron Ron" (1962), and the Shangri-Las' "Give Him a Great Big Kiss" (1964). Through listening to these American songs and considering pictures of the various groups, students will be able to identify sonic and visual markers of tropes like the "girl next door" and the "whiny, bratty girl."

More importantly, the discussion can identify the strategic value of these clichéd images. When "Will You Love Me Tomorrow?" is so clearly articulating the emotional turmoil of a girl on the brink of a first sexual encounter, it is significant that the Black singers look and sound so ordinary and relatable. The song offered girl listeners a script for articulating their trepidations and insecurities without disrupting their senses of themselves as good girls, and it used musical language so direct and non-virtuosic that listeners felt invited to join in. Analysis of this song can provide an opportunity for reflection on the politics of respectability, the constraints of being a "good girl," and the very real dangers of sex in a time before access to reliable birth control.

The Crystals' superb "Da Doo Ron Ron" (recorded in 1962) complements the Shirelles' song beautifully; not only is the galloping rhythm and "wall of sound" production thrilling to hear, but the song's use of doo wop syllables can prompt a discussion about how teens in the early 60s could articulate feelings of sexual attraction. Footage of a "live" (actually lip-synced) 1965 performance from the variety show *Shivaree* is easily found online, and this document can enable productive discussion of race.[21] The three singers of the Crystals, Black women who were aged between 18 and 21 by the time of filming their three-year-old hit, are at the center of a stage that is surrounded on all sides by audience members who are mostly white. Two white go-go dancers (one of whom, famously, is actress Teri Gaar) are prominent on platforms behind the performers, ensuring that many shots include white and Black youth together. It is striking that this kind of programming could be syndicated and broadcast into homes across the USA only five years after the violent response to six-year-old Ruby Bridges, when she became the first Black child to desegregate an elementary school in the Southern United States.[22]

"Da Doo Ron Ron" thus presents a milestone of the Civil Rights movement; furthermore, as I've argued elsewhere, the "da doo ron ron" phrase that ends each line functions as a suggestive ellipsis for what the protagonist feels but can't bring herself to say. The song uses nonsense syllables in a rapturous description of an idealized boy, presenting a "means by which girls could talk about desire without provoking outright censure."[23] When so many girl group songs are about boys, it becomes clear that the music provides a forum for sharing information about what romance feels like. It is also possible to see that, beyond a certain point, the boy himself becomes somewhat unimportant, a mere token giving girls permission to talk to one another about romantic feelings and sexual yearnings that need not always conform to the rules of compulsory heterosexuality. The value of this kind of covert language was particularly acute for queer youth in the years before Stonewall. "Da Doo Ron Ron" can thus yield many insights about how teens have managed to actualize themselves and express their desires within the restrictive confines of sexist, racist, and heteronormative expectations.

Against this backdrop, the Shangri-Las' 1964 "Give Him a Great Big Kiss" stands out for its audaciousness; in this song, the protagonist boasts about her boyfriend's charms and declares her intention to claim him publicly, by kissing him in front of his friends. Footage of the white quartet performing this song live on *Where the Action Is* can be found online; this program was a spin-off from *American Bandstand,* airing weekday afternoons from 1965 to 1967. The clip shows the singers backed by a nine-piece band, dressed alike in tight pants and white boots and modeling a rebellious style that defied propriety.[24] Lead singer Mary Weiss deploys a nasal, whiny vocal style that evokes petulance and sass, ensuring that the song sounds edgy and daring to its viewers, most of whom were children and teens watching at home after school.

The song, and the group, have often been cited as important early influences on 1970s male punk musicians such as the Ramones, and Johnny Thunders of the New York Dolls and the Heartbreakers. Although girl groups addressed themselves primarily to girl listeners, then, many boys listened as well, and learned about girls' experiences in ways that complicated their senses of their own gender. The New York Dolls performed "Give Him a Great Big Kiss" and Thunders also included it on his critically acclaimed 1978 album *So Alone,* switching gender pronouns and expressing excitement about the prospect of kissing a girl in front of her friends. While his performance maintains heterosexist norms, though, it is a striking homage to a group associated with frivolous girlhood. What is more, the song allows Thunders to perform a kind of giddy, lovestruck rapture that subverts conventional male attitudes and behaviors. Similarly, Eddie Holland, one of the all-male songwriting team of Holland, Dozier and Holland at Motown Records, commented that he liked writing lyrics for girl groups because these songs allowed him to access a broader emotional range than was permissible for a man: "We were taught coming up that you don't cry; you take it on the chin. We couldn't say we were hurt if we were hurt; we could only deal with those subjects through writing for women."[25] Girl group music thus had something to offer to listeners of many genders and ages.

Girls in Rock Culture

As fun, teen-centered rock'n'roll gave way to the more artistic ambitions and gravitas of rock culture in the late 1960s, musical depictions of the teen girl persona receded, and female-identifying artists sought to be recognized as women. Nevertheless, through the 1970s and 1980s it is possible to trace cheeky and celebratory images of girlhood, in the music of all-female bands such as the Runaways and the Go-Gos in Los Angeles, and the Slits and Bananarama in London. The Go-Gos emerged out of the Hollywood punk scene and rose to fame with their 1981 *Beauty and the Beat*, a tongue-in-cheek but ultimately heartfelt sendup of girlhood. The album included songs about gossip ("Our Lips are Sealed") and cover art depicting the band members masked in skin cream, reveling in bubble baths, and holding intense conversations on the phone. Inducting the Go-Gos into the Rock & Roll Hall of Fame in 2021, lifelong fan and movie star Drew Barrymore dressed up to recreate these photos, with a towel turban and thick white skin cream. Barrymore told the audience that *Beauty and the Beat* was the first record she bought (at age six) and that "the fact that they were girls made me feel not only invited but more important—like I could be a badass too. I looked over to my Pippi Longstocking poster on the wall and thought, Yes, I like girls who rock!"[26] With their sweet harmonies and playful style, the Go-Gos reveled unrepentantly in aspects of girl culture typically deemed mortifying, and they conferred dignity and cool on their girl listeners.

The mixed-gender band X-Ray Spex had already recorded their iconic punk track in "Oh Bondage! Up Yours!", in London in 1977, with teen singer Poly Styrene deploying a deliberately childlike voice on the opening line "Little girls should be seen and not heard, but I say: Oh bondage! Up yours!" Styrene's faux demureness contrasts brilliantly with her angry howl and the rough, raucous sounds of her bandmates' instruments. Poly Styrene offered an insubordinate, defiantly juvenile sound and stance to listeners in 1977, which contrasted significantly with the more adult, cool version of punk offered by Debbie Harry in the New York-based band Blondie that same year.

It's possible to trace a connection from X-Ray Spex to the riot grrrl style of Olympia, Washington, in the early 1990s. Participants in this scene sought very deliberately to transform the perception and experience of girlhood, infusing the notion of "girl" with a growl, and music was only one aspect of their movement. With unflinching candor, they talked openly about rape, incest, homophobia, anti-abortion activism, and other rhetoric that demeaned and harmed girls disproportionately. Riot grrls created 'zines (home-made magazines) that circulated to girls around the world. Through texts like the incendiary Riot Grrrl Manifesto, published in *Bikini Kill Zine 2* in 1991, riot grrrls called for a girl revolution "BECAUSE we are interested in creating non-hieirarchical (sic) ways of being AND making music, friends, and scenes based on communication + understanding, instead of competition + good/bad categorizations" and "BECAUSE we are angry at a society that tells us Girl = Dumb, Girl = Bad, Girl = Weak."[27] Recognizing that rock shows were often hostile, unsafe spaces for girls and women, riot grrrl bands disrupted audience conventions by insisting that male-identifying listeners stand at the back and allow "girls to the front."

Musicians in the scene, including Kathleen Hanna, whose band Bikini Kill shared a name with the 'zine she created, mobilized the aesthetic of punk to challenge the sexism and heteronormativity of contemporaneous rock culture. Songs like "Rebel Girl" (1992) celebrate the unselfconscious confidence and joy of pre-adolescent girlhood, connecting the swagger of a girl on a tricycle to the power of revolution, and using the aggressive sound of guitar distortion alongside defiantly high-pitched, girlish vocals. Hanna sought explicitly to legitimize girls' anger and inspire them to express themselves, breaking free of the restrictions that confine girls to isolated domestic spaces. Her solo 1997 album, *Julie Ruin*, was recorded in her apartment, and she later reflected that "Girls' bedrooms sometimes can be this space of real creativity. The problem is that these bedrooms are all cut off from each other. I wanted the Julie Ruin record to sound like a girl from her bedroom made this record but then didn't just throw it away, or it wasn't just in her diary, but she took it out and shared with people."[28]

Reflections and Connections: Bedroom Pop and Girlhood

This principle, and the audibly homespun, lo-fi production style of this and other riot grrrl records, connected the movement to the punk philosophy of DIY (do it yourself), and the urgency of seizing the means of (record) production even when it meant creating music that sounded unpolished by comparison with major studio releases. This idea, and esthetic, would resurface in the bedroom pop music of the late 2010s.

Artists like Clairo, Mxmtoon, Girl in Red, and Billie Eilish taught themselves to use inexpensive laptop computer programs to record and release tracks at home, without having to subject themselves to the scrutiny of music industry gatekeepers. While bedroom pop as a genre does not exclude male-identifying performers or listeners, such as Eilish's brother and collaborator Finneas Eilish, it should be recognized as a girl-led style that embraces confessional lyrics about mental health and sexuality in direct and unselfconscious songs. Artists are clear-sighted about avoiding the sexist structures and pressures of professional recording:

> "In a recording studio a lot of the time a girl or a woman could end up on the couch at the back rather than sitting at the [mixing] desk," says Marie Ulven [aka Girl in Red]. "Girls can easily end up being the ones who sit and watch. They don't do the software part as much as the boys. But I'm doing everything—including the software. Because no one else is here to do it."[29]

Through a "tour" of examples from the 1960s to the 2020s, then, it is possible to trace a history that shows how girls have used music to negotiate and resist sexism, and how they have raised their voices and found ways to communicate with one another, in defiance of social expectations and professional music institutions.

Sample Lesson Thirteen

Music and Sports

If this section of the book is broadly about the ways in which music is absorbed and made sense of, then it will be intriguing to consider some specific spaces and communities where listeners use music to forge connections. Looking beyond the obvious contexts of home listening or concert-going, we can identify many settings in which music plays a significant part and has a bearing on the shaping of gender roles. Some examples might include music and shopping, or music in the service of religious worship—here, I will offer a template for teaching about music and sport.

Music, Sports, and Masculinity

A lesson addressing sports provides an excellent way into consideration of the social construction of masculine identities, an idea that is still lamentably under-examined; the tired notion that only women have gender is akin to the thought that only non-white people have race, and both of these ideas erect barriers to the full consideration of how gender, sexuality, and race function in human experience. Within the world of sports, masculine identity characterizes our understandings of strength and achievement, as the male, presumed heterosexual, body is upheld as an exemplar in sports as different from one another as golf, hockey, and swimming. The concepts of teamwork and sportsmanship are likewise generally posited as masculine; indeed, women were until quite recently excluded from participating in sports that might render them unfeminine, and sports teams remain among the most fiercely guarded homosocial, yet homophobic, spaces still operating today.

Connections between music and sports are more considerable than might appear at first blush; your students may find it helpful to reflect that, like certain kinds of music, sports present fans with significant opportunities for community building and male bonding. Music and sports are both arenas in which identity is performed, and which share an emphasis on discipline, preparation, prowess, and competition. As with musicality, aptitude at sport may represent an opportunity for wealth and class mobility for a talented child. On the professional concert stage as on the televised tennis court, the pressure to succeed is governed by a belief that "you are only as good as your last performance." In the spheres of competitive sports as in music performance, participants must present themselves as objects of spectacle, to be scrutinized and assessed according to the beholder's gaze, and in both contexts, they may chafe at being judged for their appearance rather than purely their skill.

In a racist economy in which sports has been one of the few arenas where the strength of Black men is encouraged and celebrated, and in which music and other forms of entertainment have celebrated Black masculinity as long as it conforms to rigid stereotypes, it is particularly instructive to analyze Black manhood through the twin lenses of music and sports. As with musicians, skill and talent in sports depend on being comfortable in one's own body, on having the instincts and confidence to improvise, and on developing a keen awareness of timing, rhythm, and flow. This is most clearly legible in martial arts, and boxing in particular has multiple threads of connection to music. In North American culture, even before LL Cool J built his 1990 hit "Mama Said Knock You Out" around the metaphor of a boxing match, boxing and music have been particularly important touchstones for Black youth working to construct masculine identities imbued with strength, endurance, and power.

Boxing

It is easy to demonstrate the musicality and showmanship of boxers through the example of Muhammad Ali (1942–2016), one of the most brilliant and well-documented athletes of the 20th century. In innumerable interviews and other public speeches, Ali showed off his inventiveness with language, his facility with rhythm, and his legendary sense of timing, leading Haitian-American hip hop artist Wyclef Jean to dub him "the original rapper."[30] Through his deft wordplay almost as much as through his boxing prowess, Ali represented the strength and beauty of Black manhood in ways defiant and inspiring, remaining a durable icon of conviction and tenacity long after his days in the ring were over. Ali's life story, of course, affords insight into the major upheavals and social conflicts of the USA at mid-century: his upbringing in segregated Kentucky, his radicalization by the murder of his age-mate Emmett Till, his embrace of the Nation of Islam, and his outspoken refusal to participate in the war in Vietnam—at the cost of losing his passport, his right to fight professionally, and his title of World Heavyweight Champion—all place him at the center of 1960s activism. A class devoted to the connection between boxing and music thus permits an opportunity to teach about the USA's Civil Rights and Anti-War Movements, and to offer a valuable corrective to the negative images of Black men that continue to permeate mainstream culture.

Ali himself presents a superb example of the musicality of what Henry Louis Gates terms Signifying, a rhetorical speech style that involves "marking, loud-talking, testifying, calling out (of one's name), sounding, rapping, playing the dozens, and so on."[31] It is in Ali's sophisticated use of these techniques that Wyclef Jean notices a precursor to rapping. Ali's career also intersects with many of the important Black musicians of his generation, perhaps most notably in the historic 1974 match in Zaire, promoted as the Rumble in the Jungle and viewed on television by an estimated one billion. A three-day music festival in Kinshasa was planned to coincide with the match, featuring African American artists such as James Brown, BB King, and the Spinners, as well as African musicians including Miriam Makeba and Manu Dibango. Footage of their concerts is central to the 2008 documentary *Soul Power,* and some performances are also seen in the 1996 documentary *When We Were Kings.*

In the context of analyzing how music constructs Black masculinity, the performance of James Brown (1933–2006) is particularly useful; Brown's capacity to establish a rocksteady rhythmic groove and then play with it compares to Ali's physicality in the boxing ring. What is more, Brown's legendary dancing demonstrates an athleticism and stamina that are, in their way, on par with the work of boxers. James Brown was known by many titles, including "the godfather of soul" and "the hardest working man in show business," and he represented an ideal of Black masculinity revered far beyond his home country of the United States. Within the USA, his clout was such that, the day after Martin Luther King Jr's assassination in 1968, the city of Boston arranged for the national televised broadcast of a James Brown concert from the Boston Garden Arena, believing (correctly) that Brown could urge calm and unity in a nation reeling from this terrible loss.[32] Study of Ali and Brown in Zaire thus affords an opportunity for students to learn about two icons of Black manhood, through footage of them performing at the top of their respective games, and to consider the interconnectedness music and sport.

Of course, Brown explored many musical styles through his long career, but focus on the Kinshasa performance finds him at the peak of his heavy funk period. In this style, Brown's music focuses on groove rather than melody or harmonic direction, using melody instruments and even voices percussively, to emphasize the low end and inspire hip shaking movement. Opening his set with the revenge themed "The Payback" and finishing with the call and response anthem "Say It Loud (I'm Black and I'm Proud)," Brown led his band the J.B.s through an electrifying and exhausting show that affirmed Black Pride at every turn. With his unabashed celebration of the dancing body as an emblem of pride and power, Brown refuted notions of dance music as mindless and trivial. In so doing, he used his body and voice in improvisatory ways to present a model of Black manhood that was strong, nimble, and dazzling.

Improvisation and Individualism

The theme of improvisation and Black masculinity can be further developed through consideration of basketball's links with music, particularly jazz and hip hop. From the Harlem Globetrotters, who began performing choreographed comic routines to the tune of "Sweet Georgia Brown" at basketball games in the 1920s, to basketballer Shaquille O'Neal's four rap album releases in the 1990s, and to rapper Drake's prominent support for his hometown team the Toronto Raptors in the 2010s, the spheres of popular music and basketball intersect through their depictions of Black masculinity. In jazz, hip hop, and basketball, improvisation is a foundational skill upon which to build success, and white Canadian musicologist Ken McLeod has argued that improvisation "is central to the notion of African American identity. In its dominant social position, white society, by comparison, is relatively unaware of itself and thus perhaps less likely to find expression through improvisation."[33] Improvisation in any context is fundamentally a strategy for being creative within constraints, whether in terms of punching combinations in the boxing ring, ball-passing on the basketball court, or melodic expression over a chord progression. This analysis offers good food for discussion about the meanings of improvisation in Black and white cultural and social practices, and its function in the construction of masculine identities. Above all, the capacity to improvise is crucial to developing individuality, as being able to think on one's feet is understood as a sign of intelligence and keeping one step ahead of the rest. Students can be asked to pursue this line of thinking in relation to the role of improvisation in music genres other than jazz or hip hop; they can also be encouraged to discuss improvisation in the contexts of both femininity and non-heteronormative masculinity.

Opportunities to learn basketball, boxing, or other sports provide training in improvisation for Black boys in settler colonial societies, but we must acknowledge that girls have historically been excluded from participation. In the sphere of professional basketball, for example, the Women's National Basketball Association in the United States is particularized by gender in its name, WNBA, as distinct from the unmarked and putatively "real" and "normal" NBA. Furthermore, the financial investment in women's basketball in the US is a pittance of the moneys poured into men's basketball.[34] Yet, as African American ethnomusicologist Kyra Gaunt shows, Black girls learn improvisation through jump rope and hand clapping games, and these activities develop their strength, discipline, and musicianship in crucial ways. Through mastering the complex rhythms of the jump rope, girls practice improvising and collaborating, and their Double Dutch songs and chants serve as études for the flow and rhythmic play of hip hop. Furthermore, jump rope games have offered girls a rare opportunity to occupy public space and to demonstrate their ingenuity and athleticism within the limits of appropriate girlish behavior.[35]

Collective Identity through Sports Fandom

If a focus on improvisation leads to deeper understanding of identity formation, particularly as means of individual resistance to a backdrop of institutional racism and notions of white supremacy, then it is also instructive to consider how music forges community in the world of sports. The paradigmatic example here, particularly with regard to rituals of masculinity, is surely fan singing at football matches. Football is a globally popular sport (called soccer in the United States and Canada) that has been described as "a central ritual arena in the constitution of manhood. Through the support of a football team, the male fan affirms his status as a man (in the eyes of his peers and himself) and also articulates the nature of that manhood."[36] The compulsory masculinity and heteronormativity of attending football matches is reinforced by chants that objectify women (usually in highly sexualized terms) and that use homophobic slurs as part of the stylized aggression between fans of opposing teams.

Spectator loyalty is framed as a crucial aspect of manhood, that involves repeated performances of allegiance through group singing of insults and abuse (comparable in spirit, perhaps, to the African American expressive practice of trading insults in "the Dozens," which has long been identified as foundational to jazz musicianship). In Britain, football chants are invariably contrafacts of familiar and easy-to-sing songs, including hymns such as "Guide Me, O Thou Great Redeemer" and "Lord of the Dance" (itself a contrafact of the Shaker hymn "Simple Gifts" that is central to Aaron Copland's ballet *Appalachian Spring*) and 1960s pop songs like "Guantanamera" and "Sloop John B." Through mass singing in football arenas, cisgender and heteronormative men and boys forge a strong sense of community and belonging through the verbal abuse of their opponents.

It is irresponsible to overlook the often-spectacular destructiveness and hateful violence carried out by some football fans over recent decades. Violent behavior erupts among sports spectators around the world, of course, involving fans who are overwhelmingly male and working-class.[37] Sports rivalries seem to provide permission for displaying masculinity and letting off steam in aggressive behaviors, and they also reinforce a sense of belonging to a group. Raising their voices together in songs that celebrate the team or that taunt the opposing fans plays an important role in the rituals of masculinity in this context.

According to British folklorist Joanne Luhrs, football chants are a surviving mode of *blason populaire,* speech acts that express and reaffirm group identities and rivalries.[38] While it is easy to identify this custom as contributing to both toxic masculinity and racism (at least in Britain, where football fandom is overwhelmingly white), Luhrs helps us also to see football and *blason populaire* as defiant expressions of working class pride and dignity in the face of deindustrialization and the devaluation of skilled labor.

Reflections and Connections: Music in Other Communities

During adolescence, music allegiances are often critical to forming a coherent identity and finding one's place in a community, and particular musics are connected to specific sports. Thus, teen and pre-teen basketball players listen to music that is very different to their hockey-playing peers, and their fashion, styles of speech, and demeanor are also distinct. And while the role of music in sports may be an unfamiliar topic to those of your students who aren't interested in sports, there are many other communities in which music forges a sense of connection and group identity. Indeed, Disney's *High School Musical* franchise launched in 2006 with the premise of highly specific and separate groups of students in high school, focusing principally on the theatre kids and the athletic kids, whose worlds rarely intersected. Particular kinds of teen identity are associated with playing in the school band, for example, and the "band camp nerd" character is a cliché of other teen movies. For band kids, music offers a network of support through the turbulent and bewildering years of adolescence, and the possibility of a recognizable identity built around a specific kind of music.

Consideration of music within sports communities and adolescent cohorts can lead to a greater understanding of the complexities of masculinities in different race and class groups. Through this lesson, students can appreciate songs as documents of history and, perhaps, as texts that illuminate their own complex identities and the identities of males in their families and communities.

Discussion/Assignment Questions

1 Ask your students to consider the music loved by older women in their families. What is the appeal of these styles to those listeners? Challenge them to hear past their own prejudices and find value in that music, perhaps through a shared listening experience with an elder.
2 The persona of the effete, sophisticated and sometimes supercilious man has been linked in significant ways to music and theatre. What did this version of masculinity offer, in a time when homosexuality was illegal and frequently punishable with violence? Ask your students to consider how adopting the style and mannerisms of Noel Coward or Oscar Wilde might have been strategic for boys and men uninterested in machismo.
3 How do class, race, and other factors limit participation in riot grrrl and bedroom pop? Is home a safe space for all girls and youth?

4 1960s girl singers Lesley Gore (in the USA) and Dusty Springfield (in Britain) kept their queer sexuality secret in a time when it was not safe for a teenage girl to be out. How might the clichéd expectations of girlhood have provided safe cover for them to express themselves without provoking suspicion and censure?
5 What are other arenas, beyond the concert hall or night club, in which music serves to direct events and/or build community? Ask your students to analyze the function of music in settings familiar to them, such as a worship service.

Notes

1. Milton Babbitt, "Who Cares if You Listen?," *High Fidelity* 8/2 (February, 1958), 38–40.
2. Eric Bentley, *The Life of the Drama* (New York: Methuen, 1965).
3. Christopher Small, *Musicking: The Meanings of Performing and Listening* (Middletown: Wesleyan University Press, 1998).
4. Lisa A. Lewis, ed. *The Adoring Audience: Fan Culture and Popular Media* (New York: Routledge, 1992).
5. Judith Butler, "Performative Acts and Gender Constitution: An Essay in Phenomenology and Feminist Theory," *Theatre Journal,* 40/4 (December, 1988), 519–31.
6. Hazel Carby, *Reconstructing Womanhood: The Emergence of the Afro-American Woman Novelist* (New York: Oxford University Press, 1987), 22.
7. This idea is compellingly presented in Barbara Ehrenreich, Elizabeth Hess, and Gloria Jacobs, "Beatlemania: Girls Just Want to Have Fun," in Lisa Lewis, ed., *The Adoring Audience: Fan Culture and Popular Media* (New York: Routledge, 1992), 84–106.
8. In their 2009 song "Lisztomania," French indie pop band Phoenix invokes Liszt and his audience as they muse about discomfort with fame, so the song is not, strictly speaking, about Liszt.
9. Dana Gooley, *The Virtuoso Liszt* (Cambridge University Press, 2004): 201–35.
10. Oliver Hilmes, *Franz Liszt: Musician, Celebrity, Superstar* (New Haven: Yale University Press, 2016): 84–90.
11. Hilmes, *Franz Liszt*, 72.
12. Hilmes, *Franz Liszt*, 62.
13. Allison McCracken, *Real Men Don't Sing: Crooning in American Culture* (Durham, NC: Duke University Press, 2015).
14. McCracken, *Real Men Don't Sing*, 3.
15. For an accessible and insightful exploration of Sinatra's innovations in singing, and the impact of crooners on popular culture, see "How the Microphone Changed the Way we Sing: Cheddar Explains," https://www.youtube.com/watch?v=5gXOQ39xWz8&t=3s, accessed November 18, 2021.
16. Mitchell Morris, *The Persistence of Sentiment: Display and Feeling in Popular Music of the 1970s* (Berkeley: University of California Press, 2013): 89.

17. Morris, *Persistence of Sentiment*, 92–3.
18. Ivan Raykoff, "Liberace's Musical/Material Appeal," *Oxford Handbooks Online*, May 2018. https://www.oxfordhandbooks.com/view/10.1093/oxfordhb/9780199935321.001.0001/oxfordhb-9780199935321-e-175, accessed October 12, 2021.
19. Robert Walser, "Popular Music Analysis: Ten Apothegms and Four Instances," in Allan Moore, ed., *Analyzing Popular Music* (London: Cambridge University Press, 2003), 16–38: 37.
20. See Jacqueline Warwick and Allison Adrian, "Introduction" in Warwick and Adrian, eds., *Voicing Girlhood in Popular Music: Performance, Authority, Authenticity* (New York: Routledge, 2016): 1–11.
21. *Shivaree*, July 3, 1965, Los Angeles.
22. Among other sources, see Ruby Bridges, *This is Your Time* (New York: Delacorte Press, 2020). See also Daisy Bates, *The Long Shadow of Little Rock* (Little Rock: University of Arkansas Press, 1986). It is worth noting that six of the Little Rock Nine were girls.
23. Jacqueline Warwick, *Girl Groups, Girl Culture: Popular Music and Identity in the 1960s* (New York: Routledge, 2007): 36.
24. *Where the Action Is*, July 29, 1965. https://www.youtube.com/watch?v=01YePzk29Mc, accessed October 26, 2021.
25. Eddie Holland, cited in Charlotte Grieg, *Will You Still Love Me Tomorrow?: Girl Groups from the 50s On* (London: Virago, 1989), 134.
26. Drew Barrymore, quoted in Althea Legaspi, "Drew Barrymore Dons Go-Go's Cosplay to Induct new Wave Heroes Into Rock Hall of Fame," *Rolling Stone*, October 30, 2021. https://www.rollingstone.com/music/music-news/drew-barrymore-dons-go-gos-cosplay-to-induction-l-a-punk-heroes-into-rock-roll-hall-of-fame-1249798/, accessed February 1, 2022.
27. No author named, "Riot Grrrl Manifesto," *Bikini Kill Zine 2*, 1991. https://www.scribd.com/document/44586640/Riot-Girl-Manifesto-Eng-Ger, accessed September 29, 2021.
28. Kathleen Hanna, in *The Punk Singer*, dir. Sini Anderson, 2013.
29. Ed Power, "How Bedroom Pop Became the Dominant Sound of Gen-Y Angst," *The Independent*, December 1, 2019. https://www.independent.co.uk/arts-entertainment/music/features/bedroom-pop-billie-eilish-rex-orange-county-clairo-spotify-a9226256.html, accessed October 29, 2021.
30. Cited in Nitish Pahwa, "How One of the great Rap Collabos of the '90s Also Helped Build Muhammad Ali's Legend," *Slate.com*, March 13, 2020 https://slate.com/culture/2020/03/rumble-in-the-jungle-fugees-when-we-were-kings-history.html accessed September 4, 2021.
31. Henry Louis Gates, *The Signifying Monkey: A Theory of African-American Literary Criticism* (New York: Oxford University Press, 1988): 52.
32. David Leaf, *The Night James Brown Saved Boston*, documentary film. 2008.
33. Ken McLeod, "The Construction of Masculinity in African American Music and Sports," *American Music*, 27/2 (Summer, 2009), pp. 204–26: 222. See also McLeod's book *We are the Champions: The Politics of Sports and Popular Music* (Farnham: Ashgate, 2011).
34. https://www.wsn.com/nba/nba-vs-wnba/, accessed February 1, 2022.

35. Kyra Gaunt, *The Games Black Girls Play: Learning the Ropes from Double Dutch to Hip Hop* (New York: NYU Press, 2006).
36. Anthony King, "The Postmodernity of Football Hooliganism," *Journal of Sociology* 48/4 (December, 1997), 576–93: 585.
37. Steve Frosdick and Peter Marsh, *Football Hooliganism* (Cullompton: Willan Publishing, 2005).
38. Joanne Luhrs, "Football Chants: A Living Legacy of the 1984-85 Miners' Strike," *The International Journal of Regional and Local Studies* 3/1 (2007), 94–120.

Further Reading

Floyd, Samuel. "Ring Shout! Literary Studies, Historical Studies, and Black Music Inquiry," *Black Music Research Journal* 11/2 (Winter, 1991): 265–87.

Gaunt, Kyra. *The Games Black Girls Play: Learning the Ropes from Double Dutch to Hip Hop*. New York: NYU Press, 2006.

Levi, Ron. "Zaire '74: Politicising the Sound Event," *Social Dynamics: A Journal of African Studies* 43/2 (Winter, 2017): 184–98.

Lisa, Lewis, ed., *The Adoring Audience: Fan Culture and Popular Media*. New York: Routledge, 1992.

McCracken, Allison. *Real Men Don't Sing: Crooning in American Culture*. Durham, NC: Duke University Press, 2015.

McLeod, Ken. *We are the Champions: The Politics of Sports and Popular Music*. Farnham: Ashgate, 2011.

Small, Christopher. *Musicking: The Meanings of Performing and Listening*. Middletown: Wesleyan University Press, 1998.

Walser, Robert. "Popular Music Analysis: Ten Apothegms and Four Instances." In *Analyzing Popular Music*, edited by Allan Moore, 16–38. London: Cambridge University Press, 2003.

Carl, Wilson. *Let's Talk about Love: Why Other People Have Such Bad Taste*. New York: Bloomsbury, 2014.

Index

Achilles 72
Aladdin: Disney's *Aladdin* 90, 92, 93; pantomime character 75
Ali, Muhammad 116–117
Anderson, Marian 23, 25–26, 36n19
André, Naomi 71, 73, 95n5
Armstrong, Louis 14
Auslander, Philip 69, 95n2

Babbit, Milton 99, 121n1
Barnes, Jennifer 55
bedroom pop 113–114, 120, 122n29
Benson, Jodi 91
Bentley, Eric 99, 121n2
Bentley, Gladys 52–53, 65n24, 65n25
Berlioz, Hector 19, 35n5, 41–45, 64n4, 64n6, 64n7
Beyoncé 23
Billy Elliot 84–85
Björk 39, 61–63, 66n43, 66n44
Black Sabbath 46
blason populaire 119
Blue (album by Joni Mitchell) 56, 66n35
blues: Blues Queens 32, 39, 46–49, 53–54, 63, 64n12, 64n13, 65n16, 65n19, 65n21, 65n24, 65n26; hokum blues 51; as musical convention 27, 39, 46–49, 50, 51–52, 59
bobbysoxer 101, 105
Bonds, Estelle 24, 26, 27
Bonds, Margaret 23–25, 26, 27
Bourne, Matthew 83–84, 97n26
boxing 115–118
Brittan, Francesca, 44, 64n6

Brown, James 116–117, 122n32
Bunch, Ryan 98n41, 98n44
Butler, Judith 68, 95n1, 100, 121n5

Campbell, Elmer Simms 52
Campbell, Joseph 55, 65n30
Canon, canonical 3, 5, 6, 10, 41, 48, 102, 109
Carby, Hazel 46, 100, 121n6
Caselotti, Adriana 87, 89, 97n37
Castrati 70–73, 95n5, 95n6
Changer and the Changed (album by Cris Williamson) 30
Chauncey, George 65n22
Cheng, William 2, 11n2
Cherubino/Chérubin 74, 76, 96n13
Christian, Barbara 47, 64n10
Cinderella 86, 88–90, 98n43
Coates, Norma 22–23, 36n16
Combahee River Collective 15, 33, 35n2
countertenor 73
crooners 104–105, 121n15
Crosby, Bing 105
cross dressing 63, 73, 75
Crystals, the 110

"Dance of the Cygnets" (from Tchaikovsky's *Swan Lake*) 83
Debussy, Claude 18, 20, 35n12
Der Rosenkavalier (opera by Richard Strauss) 74–75
des Barres, Pamela 22
Dew Drop Inn 54
Disney, Walt 87–89, 93, 97n37

Index

Disney Studios 70, 85–95, 97n38, 98n44, 109
Dobkin, Alix 28–29, 30, 32, 33, 36n23, 36n24, 37n32

Eilish, Billie 114
"Empio, Dirò, Tu Sei" (from Handel's *Giulio Cesare*) 73
Falsetto 77
fatherhood 63, 84
Feldman, Maxine 28–30, 32, 36n26
feminist standpoint theory 14–15
Fleeger, Jennifer 97n38, 98n40
"Flight of the Swans" (from Tchaikovsky's *Swan Lake*) 80–81, 82, 84
Fonteyn, Margot 80
football 119, 123n36, 123n37, 123n38
Frozen 86, 94
Fuller, Sophie 16

Gates, Henry Louis 51, 116
Gaunt, Kyra 118
gender: as construct 1–3, 4–11, 13, 14, 19, 33, 35, 39, 40, 63, 68–70, 72, 73–74, 75, 76, 79, 81, 85, 86, 92, 95, 100, 111, 112, 114, 115, 118; gender-based violence 32, 43; gender binary 1, 6, 8, 29, 70, 78, 100; and genius 13, 17, 25, 26, 38, 46, 101; non-binary gender, gender transitioning 6, 15, 28, 38, 62, 76, 77–78; and sexuality 2, 27, 35, 70, 108
Giulio Cesare (opera by George Frideric Handel) 72–73, 76, 96n9
Gladstone, Mary 16
Goffman, Erving 9, 12n9, 68
Go-Gos, the 112
Goldin-Perschbacher, Shana 66n44, 66n45, 78, 97n23
Gothic 44, 45
groupies 14, 21–23, 36n16
guitar face 69

Halsey 62
Hanna, Kathleen 113, 122n28
Hardin, Lil 14

Hartsock, Nancy 14–15, 35n1
hero's quest 54–55, 91; *see also* monomyth
hooks, bell 2, 11n1, 46

I Do Not Want What I Haven't Got (album by Sinéad O'Connor) 60
Impromptu (1991 film) 18–19
intersectionality 33, 34

Johnson, Robert 48–49

Kuhn, Judy 93

Lavender Jane Loves Women 28–30
Lelkes, Anna 40
Le Nozze di Figaro (opera by WA Mozart) 74
Le Mariage de Figaro (play by Pierre-Augustin Beaumarchais) 74
lesbian, lesbianism 15, 27, 28–30, 33, 34, 36n28
Liberace 106, 107
Lilith's Fair 34
"Little Green" (song by Joni Mitchell) 56–58
Little Mermaid, The 86, 90, 91
Little Richard (Richard Penniman) 54, 65n28, 65n29
Liszt, Franz 101–104, 107, 121n9, 121n10
Lisztomania 101–103, 121n8

Madness 39, 41, 43–44, 45, 46, 64n5, 64n9
Magdalen Laundries 58–59, 66n38, 66n39, 66n40
Mahler, Alma 14
Mahon, Maureen 64n14, 65n27
"Mandy" (song recorded by Barry Manilow) 106–107
Manilow, Barry 106–107
Marvel Studios 9, 10
McClary, Susan 3, 11n6, 49, 64n13
McCracken, Allison 104, 121
Medulla (album by Björk) 61–62
Michigan Women's Music Festival 28, 31–34, 37n29
misogyny 33, 41, 42, 59

Mitchell, Joni 39, 56–59, 66n34, 66n36
monomyth 55, 59
Moreschi, Alessandro 71–72
Morris, Mitchell 106
Mulan 93
Munoz, José 70
murder ballad 42
Musicking 99, 121n3
"My Special Child" (song by Sinéad O'Connor) 60

National Association of Negro Musicians 26

Octavian 74–75, 76
O'Connor, Sinéad 39, 60–61, 66n41
Odette/Odile 79, 80–81, 82, 83, 91
Olivia Records 30–31, 36n28
Ophelia 43–44, 64n5
Orenstein, Peggy 92

pantomime 75–76, 96n16, 96n17
Pingu 7, 12
Pocahontas 90, 93
Powers, Ann 22, 36n15
pregnancy 39, 55–58, 60, 62, 64; and abortion 39, 56, 60, 64; and breastfeeding 39, 61, 62; and miscarriage 39, 60
Presley, Elvis 54, 102
Price, Florence 23–27, 36n18, 36n19, 36n20
Princess 18, 54; Disney princesses 86, 87–94, 97n38; Princess Leia 40, 45
Princess and the Frog, The 93–94

queer, queerness 16, 29, 30, 31, 38, 46, 51–54, 63, 65n22, 65n24, 65n25, 70, 78, 84, 95n3, 97n26, 97n31, 105, 111, 121

race records 49
Rainey, Ma 48, 51–52, 53, 63, 65n19
Raykoff, Ivan 107
Rhodes, Lisa 22
riot grrrl 112–113, 120

romanticism 18–19, 23, 38, 43, 45, 64n6, 78, 107
Ross, James 17–18, 35n5, 35n6, 35n7
Rumble in the Jungle, the 116, 122

Saariaho, Kaija 63–64
salon, salonnière 14, 15, 16–20, 23, 24–25, 34, 35n5, 103
Salonga, Lea 93
Sand, Georges (Aurore Dudevant) 18, 19
Schumann, Clara Wieck 13
Schwartz, Stephen 91, 98n42
scopophilia 79
Senelick, Laurence 74, 96n11
sexuality 1–6, 8, 22, 28, 33, 35, 38, 39, 44, 50, 63, 65n26, 70, 84, 86, 92, 102, 107, 108, 114, 115, 121
Shangri-Las, the 110, 111
Shirelles, the 110
Showalter, Elaine 43, 64n5
signifying 51, 54, 65, 116n17, 122n31
Silveira, Lucas 76–77, 96n19
Simonsen, Jane 3
Sinatra, Frank 105
Sleeping Beauty 86, 88–89, 92
slow teaching 3, 11n4, 38
Small, Christopher 99
Smith, Bessie 48, 49–53, 54, 64n14
Smithson, Harriet 43–44, 45
Snow White and the Seven Dwarfs 86, 87–88, 89, 90, 91, 92
Sobeshchenskaya, Anna 79–80
"Someday my Prince Will Come" (song from Disney's *Snow White and the Seven Dwarfs*) 87, 88–89
sonata form and gender 44
Spoon, Rae 78
Springfield, Dusty 121
Star Wars 9, 40–41, 54
Stonewall 28, 111
Strauss, Richard 10, 74
Styrene, Poly 112
Swan Lake 78–85, 97n25, 97n26, 97n31, 97n32, 97n33; *Barbie: Swan Lake* 82
Symphonie fantastique 38, 39–45

Tagaq, Tanya 61
TallBear, Kim 5–6, 11n7
Tchaikovsky, Pyotr Ilyich 20–21, 35n11, 35n12, 36n13, 36n14, 78, 81, 83, 107
Tillery, Linda 31, 32, 36n28
Tilson-Thomas, Michael 42
Trans Exclusionary Radical Feminism (TERF) 28, 33
travesti 70, 71, 73–75, 95n5, 96n13

Vallée, Rudy 104–105, 106, 107
Vienna Philharmonic Orchestra 40
Viardot, Pauline 19–20

von Meck, Nadezhda 20–21, 35n12, 36n13

Wagner, Cosima Liszt 14
Wagner, Richard 18, 19, 104
Walser, Robert 3, 11n3, 46, 108, 122n19
White, Portia 26–27
Whiteness 8–10, 15, 25–26, 31–32, 109, 110, 115, 118, 119
Williams, John 10, 40–41, 93
Williamson, Cris 30, 32
Woman's Symphony Orchestra of Chicago 25
women and music 1, 25

For Product Safety Concerns and Information please contact our EU representative GPSR@taylorandfrancis.com
Taylor & Francis Verlag GmbH, Kaufingerstraße 24, 80331 München, Germany

www.ingramcontent.com/pod-product-compliance
Lightning Source LLC
Chambersburg PA
CBHW051752230426
43670CB00012B/2250